TAROT SPREADS

A Beginner's Guide to Reading Tarot Cards

(An Introduction to the Secrets of Tarot Card Reading)

Jeffrey Price

Published by Sharon Lohan

© **Jeffrey Price**

All Rights Reserved

Tarot Spreads: A Beginner's Guide to Reading Tarot Cards
(An Introduction to the Secrets of Tarot Card Reading)

ISBN 978-1-990334-65-8

All rights reserved. No part of this guide may be reproduced in any form without permission in writing from the publisher except in the case of brief quotations embodied in critical articles or reviews.

Legal & Disclaimer

The information contained in this book is not designed to replace or take the place of any form of medicine or professional medical advice. The information in this book has been provided for educational and entertainment purposes only.

The information contained in this book has been compiled from sources deemed reliable, and it is accurate to the best of the Author's knowledge; however, the Author cannot guarantee its accuracy and validity and cannot be held liable for any errors or omissions. Changes are periodically made to this book. You must consult your doctor or get professional medical advice before using any of the suggested remedies, techniques, or information in this book.

Upon using the information contained in this book, you agree to hold harmless the Author from and against any damages, costs, and expenses, including any legal fees potentially resulting from the application of any of the information provided by this guide. This disclaimer applies to any damages or injury caused by the use and application, whether directly or indirectly, of any advice or information presented, whether for breach of contract, tort, negligence, personal injury, criminal intent, or under any other cause of action.

You agree to accept all risks of using the information presented inside this book. You need to consult a professional medical practitioner in order to ensure you are both able and healthy enough to participate in this program.

Table of Contents

INTRODUCTION 1

CHAPTER 1: TAROT 3

CHAPTER 2: COMMON TAROT SPREADS 29

CHAPTER 3: HOW SELF DEVELOPMENT WITH THE TAROT WORKS 42

CHAPTER 4: KNOW THY FRIEND 51

CHAPTER 5: ALL YOU NEED TO KNOW ABOUT THE MAJOR ARCANA 72

CHAPTER 6: BEGINNING YOUR FIRST READING. 86

CHAPTER 7: SUIT OF SWORDS 98

CHAPTER 8: WANDS 104

CHAPTER 9: KNOWING MORE ABOUT THE MINOR ARCANA CARDS 109

CHAPTER 10: HOW TO READ TAROT SPREADS 128

CHAPTER 11: COMMON TAROT READING MISTAKES 135

CHAPTER 12: 10 TOP DECKS TO CONSIDER WHEN BUYING TAROT CARDS 145

CHAPTER 13: THE SYMBOLICAL TAROT THE FIRST SEPTENARY: 1 TO 6 ARCANA: THEOGONY 157

CONCLUSION 194

Introduction

This book has actionable steps and strategies on how to do tarot card reading for a happier and more fulfilling life.

Have you watched movies where there was tarot card reading and you wondered what the heck was that? Did you find this interesting and want to learn a thing or two about tarot reading? Do you want to learn but are not sure where to start? If this is you, then this is the perfect book for you.

This book explains in simple language what tarot is, the 78 tarot cards used in tarot as well as the meanings of the different individual cards as well as a combination of different cards. You will learn how to ask a question, shuffle, cut and deal cards as well as some common spreads used by tarot card readers.

Thanks again for downloading this book, I hope you enjoy it!

Chapter 1: Tarot

What are Tarot Cards?

These set of cards are one of the most misunderstood cards ever. Quite frankly, tarot cards are just a set of playing cards. Yes, you read right, and it's still being played in a lot of countries in Europe. Basically, as a player, you must trump if you're left with no cards and tarot games are usually point-trick games. Each card has a value which depends on the game.

Tarot cards have a separate 21-card trump suit, and in addition, there's also a card called the Fool. Just like the joker, its use depends on the game being played. It's either the trump card or some card that you won't include in the game. Initially, the game played using the tarot cards was called triumph and it's very similar to the modern game bridge.

There are some people who might scoff at the idea that one can understand their past, present or the future through a deck of cards. You might also have found it strange initially. You might have judged the people who had believed this had lost their minds. But that is where you are wrong!

The cards have actually been proved accurate. You will be able to understand yourself better. You will also be able to learn how to deal with the different challenges that you might face in your future. Tarot cards have similarities and dissimilarities with a deck of cards it has numbers, letters, courtly kings and queens, plus suits.

However, tarot cards are not for playing. Its use borders on the divinity with graphic representations of energies and events that people are likely to encounter in life, like decision-making, reflection, heartache, togetherness, joy leaving things behind, new beginnings, patience, determination, and so much more.

A tarot deck contains 78 different cards, where the majority of which are referred to as the minor arcana and 22 are known as the major arcana. The major arcana portrays the significant changes in your life path. Some of the similarities of a deck of tarot cards with your usual deck of cards are that both have four different types of suit and they are even-numbered from one to ten, followed by page, knight, queen, and king.

There are decks that make use of prince and princess for their page and knight. For the tarot, these suits are: the pentacles, which denote the earth or the physical world; the swords, which indicate the air or the mind; cups which mean water or emotions; and wands which denote fire or the spirit. These suits and numbers are only seen within the 56 cards of the minor arcana. There are also tarot decks that use different names for their suits.

Basically, tarot cards can be used as a divining tool through the reading of the tarot spread and interpretation of the card interactions from the spread, the layout of the cards in each spread in relation to your life's current issues or issues of importance to you. It can help you assess your life situation, how you can go about present obstacles that you are facing, however it cannot make decisions for you. Tarot readings are not carved in stone, a lot of things can still affect the situation, but it is there to help you gauge your strengths and weaknesses in order to come up with the right solution.

I know you may have heard of various uses that people have put tarot reading into, so let us tackle them all here and clear the myth and the illusion that shroud this divinity tool.

Many people have turned to tarot card reading for hopes of getting a glimpse of their future. Yes, tarot can provide roadmaps to your future, but it can never provide definitive answers.

However, if you follow your current course s of action, it can tell you what is likely to happen. Furthermore, a tarot reader can also be clairvoyant, he or she could tell that there are three kids in your future, however the action still falls upon your shoulder if you want to act on it or not.

It would be much more useful if the reading can help you to examine your life more closely, like what is going on subconsciously? How can you make things better for yourself? How are you approaching your social life, your family or your work? The tarot reading can help you to throw light on things that were previously far from the obvious and to understand yourself better.

Through this, it will be these 'eureka' moments when you understand better why you felt like that and will wonder why you didn't think of it before.

Commonly, many people used tarot readings as a way to get an answer for a current life situation that they need help deciding with. Some may have questions that are answerable with a yes or a no—and if this is the case with you, why not toss a coin? Heads for yes and tails for a no. But, you won't right? Because you also want to know the reason behind each answer. Tarot reading can help on this matter; however, it does not have a yes or a no card. But, tarot reading can help you clarify the subject through the understanding of related issues which will then allow you to reach a decision.

Tarot reading is more of making an informed choice instead of finding definitive answers. It is all about making use of the insights that you have gained through the cards to reach your own conclusion or decision.

The purpose you hold when reading your tarot spread is crucial. It can be very enticing to just swiftly scan a tarot spread, look up their brief meanings and move on to make the next tarot spread because you felt that the first one didn't apply much to your current situation.

If you do tarot readings this way, then you will always have shallow answers to your questions, however if you spend time trying to understand what each card is telling you, and later you will arrive at a deeper meaning. Often times, it is also good to reflect on the tarot spread that you have received for a day, and you just might see that the answers that you will arrive to will be more revealing and a little more in-depth.

Through time, your attitude towards your card will influence your relationship with them. If you give your card the due respect for what it can teach you, then answers that you get out of them will be more meaningful.

Safety of Tarot Cards

Many people are concerned that tarot cards are evil because they can be a way of channeling evil spirits or harm. What you need to understand is that, a reader only uses the tarot cards as a divinity tool, just as any driver would use a car. If the driver is under no influence of alcohol, chances are he won't be channeling harm.

On the other hand, the vehicle also has a positive tool; you can bring the whole family to faraway places that generally would not be possible.

Therefore, it is the tarot reader who actually holds these channels of good and bad vibes. So, it is also prudent that if you want a tarot reader, look for one whom you can trust. Before you begin seeing a tarot reader, ask yourself are you comfortable telling the reader your secrets or paying them money? If you have difficulty trusting the tarot reader, then chances are you better off without a reading.

When you allow somebody to read your tarot spread you are essentially providing them a glimpse into your personal life, for it to be examined at will and leisure on the table. You are also providing the reader with the power to tell you what they see. Now, there is no real danger to all that—the REAL danger lies on what how they tell you what they are seeing and HOW you are going to perceive this and apply it to your current life.

For example, if a tarot reader is a bitter person when it comes to love because of past and personal experiences, she or he may impart this bitterness to you. She or he may carelessly but unintentionally tell you inappropriate things like there is no future in your current relationship. This could leave you feeling with little hope for the future of your ten-year marriage, lost or confused.

A responsible tarot reader would explore their cards more and try to comment to get more from you instead of divulging inappropriate things. The responsible tarot reader could rephrase her response to you by saying there is a lack of communication between you and your partner... or I can sense that you are not fully open with your partner, why is this?

All in all, a tarot reader cannot definitively decide for you, all the decisions lie on you. Saying that your relationship has no future is denying you to look at the whole picture and can then prod you to get a divorce. When in fact, you do have a choice, stay and repair the relationship or get out. But, the way the cards were conveyed to you by the reader does matter and may mean that you need to get a divorce which can be dangerous since it will cause chaos in your life. Used that way, the tarot reader can also be a channel for bad things.

Tarot History and Evolution

The precise origins of the tarot are not known. There are sources that point to Buddhism and India and there is also evidence that point to playing cards used in the 11th century in China. However, the most likely theory is that, the tarot can be traced to the priesthood in Egypt that used these cards.

The tarot survived various eras hidden in church walls and at other times used as a gaming tool. It was relatively unchanged until the 19th century where new and several tarot decks were made. Since the production of tarot cards was small scale, this also limited its circulation—leaving it only in the hands of individuals who are highly active in the occult.

By 1910, the first-ever commercial deck produced was made by A. E. Waite, the tarot cards came to be known as the Rider-Waite Deck. Almost all known modern versions of the tarot cards are based on this deck. Due to the modern printing methods and ease of access, tarot reading grew in popularity. It has been quite accessible to anyone who wants to explore the use of tarot, however not all understand tarot because this only comes with personal growth and continuous study.

It should be noted that the origin of tarot cards remains a mystery. However, we do know that in the 15th century – the Italians made use of these cards in a popular game card game. The wealthy people of the society commissioned beautiful decks. It is amazing to know that some of them have survived.

The eighteenth and nineteenth-century marked the discovery of these cards by the influential scholars of occult. The cards fascinated these gentlemen and they came to the conclusion that the images on the cards were more than just a game. They had powerful meaning and idea behind them.

This leads them to reveal (or create) the history of tarot. In this regard, they primarily connected the cards to the Hermetic philosophy, Egyptian mysteries, alchemy, the Kabbalah and other mystical systems. It should be noted that these pursuits were a significant part of the 20th century and were incorporated in various societies.

The roots of the tarot lie in the occult tradition, however the interest started to increase only in the last few decades. Over time, people have developed various perceptions and propositions about the tarot cards. In this regard, new cards have also been created. This is mainly due to the multifaceted interests of people belonging to different areas.

There are different types in this regard. For example,

Native American

Dragon

Herbal

Japanese Deck

An interesting this to note is that tarot is commonly perceived as a tool for divination. The conventional mode of tarot reading involves two parties.

Seeker – Someone who wants answers to personal questions

Reader – Someone who has the knowledge of interpreting the cards

The seeker shuffles and cuts the deck. This step is followed by the laying out of the chosen cards. It should be noted that the cards are laid out in a specific pattern which is called spread. One of the exciting things to mention here is that each position of the spread holds a different meaning. Moreover, each card has a different meaning too.

The reader concludes the final meaning based on the pattern of spread and the meaning of each card. During the complete process, the reader is guided by spiritual communication or psychic intuition.

At this point, you should note that it's not essential to be psychic in order to read tarot successfully. On the other side of the picture, there is another proposition which states that you develop the qualities of psychic with training and practice. However, the case may differ based on the belief system of a person. You only need a little bit of intuition to read tarot cards effectively.

How Can I Use Tarot Cards?

Tarot is great in helping you make choices, manifesting goals, writing a book planning a business, coaching others, meditating—you name it. Tarot card reading enables you to:

Pay Attention to Your Intuition

Tarot card reading is an extremely personal endeavor and the meanings locked within the cards vary from person to person and from one query to another. The same card could hold an entirely different meaning for you than what it had for your friend because you are different people with different identities and intuition. This is the beauty of tarot cards; it talks to you about yourself and your life. This is how it helps you become more intuitive and understand the incredible power of your mind.

Better Comprehend Threats and Opportunities

Tarot cards enable you to have a better awareness of your past, present and future as well as your behavior and personality so you can better understand whether a specific person, thing, idea, event or situation is a threat or an opportunity for you, which will ensure you make wiser decisions accordingly.

Stay on Guard and Take Risks at the Right Time

If you learn to read tarot cards, you can soon become equipped with the power to understand and explore the hidden meaning associated with things so you know when to stay on guard and when to do something uncertain that can yield excellent results for you.

Dig Deeper into Your Genuine Aspirations

Luckily, tarot can change things around for you. The cards based on your desire to know yourself and your heart's deepest desires can give you meaningful answers about who you are and what you should really be doing so you can then pursue exactly what you want and add more structure to your boring life.

Make Sense of Your Purpose in Life

As you start becoming more aware of what you want in life, what you should do, the threats you need to avoid and the opportunities you should grab on to, you start to make better sense of your life and your purpose in it. What is next then? Well, you then simply find out meaningful ways to go about that route so you can fulfill your purpose and live each day with meaning and happiness.

Tarot and Occult correspondences

As we had emphasized, it is always better to explore surrounding cards to get a more comprehensive insight. Most often, the message becomes clearer if all the cards are interpreted and viewing them from a broader perspective. Try to see how they relate to each other or if they have something in common?

Tarot practitioners are adding correspondence elements to arrive at a particular interpretation of cards such as Numerology and Astrology. The Elements of Fire, Water, Air, and Earth have astrological associations that are significant when you read the count cards.

Here are some of these similar associations.

Pentacles: Capricorn, Virgo, and Taurus

Swords: Sagittarius, Aries, and Leo

Wand: Aquarius, Libra, and Gemini

Cups: Scorpion, Pieces, and Cancer

Depending on the Styles and tradition used by tarot practitioners, along with the school of thoughts where sign and element correspondents vary, there are many variations on the astrological associations and other correspondence.

Pentacles Element - Earth (Matters that deal with money, protection, securities, and practical concerns)

Wands Elements - Air (Matters that deal with intellect, intelligence, thoughts, and ideas)

Swords Element - Fire (Matters that pertain to action, power, purification, energy, and transformation)

Cups Element - Water (Matters that deal with emotions and subconscious, dreams, and creativity.

There is a common understanding that Wands are the elements of fire while the swords are of the air, but this is subject to contemplation as wood is the primary component of Wands. Woods come from trees whose branches gently moved air attributing it to that element, and same with the Sword forged in fire.

Tarots mechanics

You and every other human being, is always scared or hesitant to receive any message. Human beings were not born optimists. If someone walks up to them and says that they have a message to deliver to them, they will worry that it is something terrible.

They start wishing that they would not have to listen to the message at all! But, when you are ready to receive messages from the universe, you will find that there is a message in every tiny entity that exists in the universe. You will find that the meaning you are looking for actually gives you the objective of every entity. This is why it is often called a mystery that can only be discovered when the outer and inner realities connect.

You will find that every Tarot card has a meaning of its own and provides you with connections that will give you the meaning behind life. You will only be able to understand the meaning behind the images if you are ready to perceive the meaning behind these cards.

Many psychics and mediums believe that the meaning behind the cards from a Tarot reading comes from deep within us. It has been mentioned above that it is your unconscious that helps you identify the meaning behind a Tarot reading. This is the perfect guide to you since it knows you very well. It goes by many names – the Inner guide, the soul, and the higher self – and has a great connection with the Tarot.

Every human being has this guide within them. There are quite a few people out there who have tried to sever the connection that exists between them and their unconscious; they have never succeeded.

You will find that you can only ignore what your subconscious is telling you! But, when you are reading the Tarot cards, you will find yourself drawing meaning from your unconscious. This is the only way by which you will be able to impart wisdom through Tarot reading. The unfortunate thing is that most people trust their conscious mind to help them find the true meaning of the cards. They forget to dig deeper.

You will find meaning when you read the Tarot cards only if you are willing to give yourself up to your unconscious. You will find yourself interpreting the meaning behind the cards and will be able to make the right choices for you and for the people around you in any given situation. You have to acknowledge the fact that you do not need the Tarot cards alone to reach your unconscious. You will need to tap into it much before you begin to read the Tarot.

Chapter 2: Common Tarot Spreads

There are many spreads used for tarot reading. Of those the Celtic cross spread and the Yin and Yang spread are the most famous. The Three Card Spread is the easiest and the most basic of the different types of spreads.

The Three Card Spread

The three-card spread is the easiest spread for Tarot reading. This spread is the perfect spread when you want to have an insight into the past, present and the future. Although the tarot cannot predict the future, it provides some insights into your feelings at a future date. It is a best option to master the three-card spread before you venture into the other two spreads mentioned in this chapter.

You will have to spread the three cards that are drawn in the following way.

The card in the center tells you about yourself – the way you feel at that particular moment. The card to the left tells you about the different opportunities and obstacles that might come your way. The last card, the card to the right, helps you identify a solution to your problem.

Celtic cross Spread

The Celtic cross is the most popular pattern used during Tarot reading. The layout is very simple but holds a great amount of power. There is a very strong energy around this spread. This is due to the fact that it has been used by several secret societies over the last few decades.

Cross/Circle Staff

The Celtic cross is divided into two parts – the Circle or cross where six cards are placed and the staff where four cards are placed. The Cross / Circle is a simulation of the Celtic cross that is found in Ireland. This cross has a circle that links the spokes, which are perpendicular to each other. This symbolizes the connection between the spirit and the matter of all beings and events that happen in time. The energies of the circular section are feminine, which work in unison with the energy of the staff section that is masculine.

The two parts of the Celtic cross are mirror images of the duality of nature. They depict the polarities found in the human psyche.

The Circle / Cross has two crosses – the smaller one which is in the center consisting of two cards which is enclosed in the bigger cross consisting of six cards. The small cross depicts the event that is most connected to you at the time of the reading. The larger cross shows how the events have occurred from your past to your future that is the card to the far left depicts your past while the card to the far right of the cross depicts your future. The cards at the top of the cross depict your conscious mind while the cards at the bottom of the cross depict your unconscious. The cards in the Staff section talk about your life and they usually do not deal with the present. To interpret the meaning of the cards in the Celtic cross spread you have to let yourself be guided by your unconscious. You will be able to understand your future better and also help people understand their future better.

How to interpret the meaning of the positions in the spread

There are ten positions in the spread. The following section covers how one can interpret the meaning of the cards from these positions.

Position 1

The first position is the center of the Circle / Cross. It is the card that is lying at the bottom. The card at this position helps you identify the problem at hand. It also depicts your worries and fears. The card helps you identify how you are coping with the situation at hand. It also helps you understand how the situation is affecting you personally.

Position 2

The second position is the card at the center of the Circle / Cross. The card at this position helps you identify the factors that are causing the problem. It also helps you identify the consequences of the problem at hand.

Position 3

This card is the one right below the center of the Cross/ Circle. This card helps you identify the heart of the problem. It tries to analyze the problem and look at the larger picture.

Position 4

This position is to the left of the center in the Circle / Cross. The card tries to identify whether there is any incident from your past that is affecting your current problem. It also helps you identify the experiences that you might have to let go off in order to forge ahead in life.

Image Courtesy: Rafael Penaloza

Position 5

This position is to the top of your center. The card tells you about your aims in life. It helps you identify your moral values and judgments. It also helps you identify if there are any changes that you have to make in your attitude in order to lead a better future.

Position 6

This position is to the right of the center of the Circle / Cross. The card tells you what you can expect from the future. It signifies the influence that a person or entity might have on you. This card also tells you what attitude you have to adopt to have a happy future.

Position 7

This position is the bottom of the Staff. It tells you exactly about you! You will learn things about yourself that you would not have thought of before. It tells you all you need to know about you – your appearance, point of view, and way of being. It tells you about their self – esteem as well!

Position 8

This position is the second from bottom in the Staff. The card at this position tells you about the environment surrounding you. It tells you how others perceive you around you.

Position 9

This position is the second from the top in the Staff section of the Celtic cross. The card at this position tells you what characteristics of yourself you need to change. You might also have to change your beliefs in order to understand the problem better. It guides you to help you understand your hopes and fears.

Position 10

This position is the top of the staff in the Celtic cross. It gives you a solution to your problem and also tells you about the outcome of that solution. It tells you how you will perceive the solution and what consequences – good or bad – you might face because of the solution.

Yin Yang spread

The Yin and Yang spread throws light on a situation where the people concerned have an issue with each other. It could also be used when a person has conflicting emotions about a certain aspect in life. These people might not necessarily be against each other but they disagree on a lot of matters. Sometimes they need to look elsewhere to find the solutions to their problems. The Yin Yang theory is based on the Chinese symbol of the Yin and the Yang – a circular shape made by two symbols, one black and the other white, divided by a central line.

The opposing Sides

In this spread, the cards depict the opposing sides of the problem. The cards on the left (3 – 5 – 7 – 9) represent side A while the cards on the right (4 – 6 – 8 – 10) represent side B. While using this spread during tarot reading, you place the cards alternately, that is you place one card on the left and one card on the right. You do this till you place all eight cards. Remember to first select the two groups, that is Side A and Side B.

The dividing line defines the point at which the opposing sides meet. The cards 1 and 2 define the problem itself, the fundamental issue. The key to the conflict is held by Card 11, which is the bottommost card in the dividing line. The Card 12 projects the outcome, which is the topmost card in the dividing line. The cards in the center of the dividing line are the cards numbered 1 and 2. The following section covers the importance of the position of the spread of cards.

How to interpret the meaning of the positions in the spread

The positions are similar to the positions in the Celtic cross spread.

Card 1 and 2 / Position 1and 2

These cards tell you about the source of the problem. The cards also show you the influences of external factors on the problem at hand.

Card 3 / Position 3

This card tells you the position of Side A in the problem. It also tells you the perception that Side B has for Side A.

Card 4 / Position 4

This card tells you the position of Side B in the problem. It also tells you the perception that Side A has for Side B.

Card 5 / Position 5

It tells you about the outcome that Side A would like to obtain.

Card 6 / Position 6

It tells you about the outcome that Side B would like to obtain.

Card 7 / Position 7

This card depicts the unconscious understanding to the problem on behalf of Side A.

Card 8 / Position 8

This card depicts the unconscious understanding to the problem on behalf of Side B.

Card 9 / Position 9

This card provides guidance to Side A on how to approach the problem or situation at hand.

Card 10 / Position 10

This card provides guidance to Side B on how to approach the problem or situation at hand.

Card 11 / Position 11

This card provides guidance to both parties on how they should overcome the conflict.

Card 12 / Position 12

The card in this position provides you with the solution to the problem.

Chapter 3: How Self Development With The Tarot Works

You can think about why you want to read tarot cards, and you can focus on the things that help tarot cards reading, what you have in mind. Try asking a question before you see the tarot reader. Do not think that Tarot Cards are designed to match yes or no. If you see the leadership in the Tarot from the reader, you can also feel better at the end of the session. Also, ask reasonable questions. You can also have a clearer view of how to see further into the future.

Some may feel as if Tarot has helped to overcome the situation, which could stand in the presence of life and may eventually see a change. Numbers can be useful in some decisions in your life. They can lead you. Some people need guidance only for a short time when collecting ideas. There are many interpretations of some tarot cards.

Even if you are a beginner, you can still read tarot cards. The best resources you can find on the internet regarding the type of Tarot that you want to use, whether it be online, face to face, or by email, CD or tape, or even books. There are also various articles available for reading in all of the above items that you can refer to. The sites are available for anyone to check out the different and variable Tarot Cards. Tarot cards for centuries claim that they offer or even help to answer all the provocative questions in life.

Tarot cards have advantages and limitations. Everyone decides no matter where he is in his life. Tarot does not work miracles and does not replace any medical care and other medications. Tarot cannot physically help you with any problem that you may have; they can only guide you. They cannot answer whether you will marry or have a child on a given day or date.

There are different sets of cards, depending on the type of Tarot card or packages that you can read. If you are interested in reading tarot cards, you can always search the internet for more questions that you can lay on the cards. Tarot cards can be very accurate in terms of events or what happened to this person. The Internet is the fastest way to find out more information about tarot cards.

Tarot data is available to people if they need to contact them and compare them by images or numbers on tarot cards. People can be emailed Tarot Cards. It is entirely up to the individual if they want to know by different methods. There's an encyclopedia on tarot cards.

You can also do a personal journal once the Tarot is being taught, and maybe a reflection of what a person did in this life is the way of life.

There are also courses that can be taught on tarot cards. There are many websites that can be checked; also, many pictures of tarot cards can be seen on them as well.

There are many decks or tarot cards that can vary around the world; it serves many purposes in your life and journey. Tarot has a confusing history. Cards can always be studied on the course, if possible. The results of tarot cards can be achieved by analyzing the card. Tarot cards can be a good thing when you focus on what you're thinking right now. Good luck reading the Tarot. Bring more tarot messages.

What is Paranormal Tarot Cards Reading?

The history of paranormal Tarot Cards is something that is disguised by time. There are some testimonials and scientists who combine the source of the Tarot with that of ancient Egypt. At the same time, other teachers and the researchers suggest that the spelling of the sources of happiness with a very ancient bohemian refinement. However, more scientists add an Italian source to the tarot cards, and it is believed that Tarot cards have become psychic tools near 1400. From this experience, many different types have evolved and are only used now. One of the popular Bridges is the Rider-Waite Bridge.

A typical tarot deck contains 78 cards consisting of the four seeds seen in normal card games, which are hearts, diamonds, shovels, and clubs. The Latin version of the tarot game has a different set of outfits.

These are swords, batons, mugs, and coins. Like a normal game, the tarot cards are numbered from one to ten plus four court cards, jack, queen, king, and Ace.

The difference between the tarot deck and the regular deck is 21 divine cards known as major Arcans. The equivalent tease in the game Tarot is called a fool, or an excuse. A fool can take all four seeds and act as the strongest good.

Reading a tarot card is easy because each trump card has a separate meaning. However, if you want to read the meaning of collecting cards, you need to make an interpretation. These maps have astrological links to data located in the context of the Octavian calendar. It is believed that tarot cards easily describe the physical and emotional characteristics of the subject.

The rich and centuries-old tradition of tarot reading is constantly evolving over time. Methods of interpretation of tarot cards continue to develop to achieve the culture in which they live. Changing the meaning can also contribute to the development of the Charter itself. Elements of the Tarot Card today are very different from what they were before.

Many tarot data are done face to face. You can find someone who reads tarot cards in your area by doing an online search, check local ads, or asking in an occult library. You should come prepared with a question or query much of the time, and you may find that if you can get useful ideas from the reading, it is more of a perceptive tool than a truly esoteric tool. Each Tarot reader has his own preferences on how to arrange cards and read them; however, one can reasonably expect that more complex and longer reading will be more expensive.

You can also have tarot reading on your phone. If you cannot find a local person who makes tarot reading or prefer extra discretion, it may be a good choice. Although you should expect that reading tarot on your phone will be quite expensive, avoid questionable minute-by-minute billing services. There are reliable Tarot readers who provide data over the phone at a reasonable flat rate. Some may also offer online readings for a small amount, and provide their interpretation of the maps through email.

Tarot cards have existed for centuries and have been used in many cultures for divination purposes. There are different card layouts, and there are different card reading methods that card readers use. The interpretation of Tarot Cards is based on the position of the card and the different symbols of each card.

Chapter 4: Know Thy Friend

As I said, starting with this chapter, we will focus on the art of tarot reading as such: what you need to do and how to interpret an answer for yourself or for another seeker. Thus, we need to begin with the meanings of each individual card. There are 78 cards in a normal deck and they are divided in two large categories: the Major Arcana (22 cards) and the Minor Arcana (56). Each of these has its own purpose: while the Minor Arcana is primarily used for daily, frequent questions, and readings, the Major Arcana usually serves to provide answers for more important, higher charged problems.

I will present here the meanings that were, over time, attributed to each of the cards. However, always keep in mind that these are not the only possible ways in which you can interpret an answer if one of these cards shows up. Moreover, as I mentioned at an earlier point, these (should) will serve just as your guide in the first period of practice. In time, you will see that you will form your own interpretations. Also, the person or the problem in front of you must always be taken into consideration. Always try to adapt the signs, the name, and the colors on a card according to the specifics of a certain context. Until then, let's see what history has to teach us.

Major Arcana

00 – The Fool. The general interpretation of this card is that of positive change, newness, innovation, and even purity and innocence. In love, this might be a sign that you are not yet ready for a long commitment, and that the time has not yet come for you to settle down; there are still many experiences for you to have. In work, this can be related to a positive change in position, but which might attract some doubts or lack of confidence from the others. In terms of health, this card is usually associated with a fragile condition, while, in finance, this can be a sign that you should follow your instinct, because a good profit is waiting for you.

01 – The Magician. This is a positive card, given the fact that it's usually associated with power, and the ability to make an important change (as in improvement) in your life. You have this power (physically, mentally and spiritually) and this is the right moment to do it. You should follow your intuition in every area of life (love, work place and finance). You may also try to enter into a deeper spiritual study of yourself in order to get to know your full potential, which might not have been discovered yet.

02 – The High Priestess. On the opposite corner is the High Priestess; this card has "darker" connotations, because it is usually associated with something negative; what is hidden – our concealed unconscious. However, this is important to maintain the balance with the everyday reality – the palpable. Thus, this is sign that the seeker must look for double meanings, and mysteries, which can also be shown in your dreams. Pay attention to the messages that the unconscious tries to send to you. In love, this card tells you that you can follow your instincts. In the other areas, always remember to consider everything from more perspectives.

03 – The Empress. This card is usually associated with motherhood, the endless power of a woman, and even with the almighty nature. This means stability, abundance of resources, wisdom, and caring. It can also be interpreted as a proper time for marriage and motherhood (pregnancy).

04 – The Emperor. Just like the father figure that we are all used to, this card is a sign of authority, dominance, rule-orientation, domination of the mind over the soul, and self-control. It can mean that you need these values in your life, and you must take this need into consideration, or that there is already such a person in your proximity, and that you should pay attention to his (her) role in your life. Be more organized in all the aspects of your life that are not developing as you would like them to.

05 – The Hierophant. This card is in connection to the need for spirituality, of knowing that you are doing the right thing, seeking confirmation, and wisdom. Also, you might feel the need of religious guidance in order to make sure that you are on the right track. And this is precisely what you should do. Search for a person who represents this sense of correctness, morality, and spiritual knowledge. In the other areas of life, make sure that, at least for the time being, you follow the rules, stick to the traditional ways, and avoid spontaneous decisions.

06 – The Lovers. This can be interpreted as a need to find personal and sexual union with another person, usually after a period when the seeker was mainly centered on their own problems. However, it should also make them think about how their problem might be related to ambivalence, a struggle to find the middle path between two options (one belonging to the heart, and the other, to the mind). The answer in this case would be whatever is closer to your heart.

07 – The Chariot. After a long and difficult struggle, the one who knows how to use all his / her tools is the one to enjoy the sweet taste of successful achievements. This is what this card represents. If the seeker is currently in a difficult period, and has doubts regarding the fate of his / her efforts, this card is a sign that everything will pay off in the end. Thus, perseverance, effort, and ambition should characterize you in this period.

08 – Strength. This card can be related to a more troubled period, one of challenges, and needs in which you need power, optimism, control of the self, and of the others. And these are the qualities that you should seek for if you want to solve the present problems. This is also a sign of stability and balance, usually with a positive interpretation.

09 – The Hermit. After looking for power and strength on the outside, now it seems like the right time to search for truth in yourself. It is (or should be) a period dedicated to introspection, and reflection on your own evolution. Also, this may be a sign that you need spirituality in your life, and the necessity to feel that you are at peace with yourself and your own decisions and choices.

10 – The Wheel of Fortune. Just like the name says, this card corresponds to a moment of constant change, but a change that must be seen in a positive light. You can now reach the culmination of a long-term situation that you have wondered about where it could lead you. Unlike the other cards predicting change, this one is about something that will come with or without your effort or even conscious wish. Let yourself carried by the power of fate, and don't try to fight the newness in any aspect of your life. Although you may not be able right now to understand it, you will eventually see that a new stage / cycle has begun, and you don't have to fear it.

11 – Justice. This card shows the need for balance (personal, professional, and spiritual). You might also be facing a turning point in your life, when you must make sure that you make the best decisions, that both take into account the past and prepare you for the future. Another interpretation would be that someone or something in the outside world needs you to be fair, considerate, and equilibrated in relation to a problem.

12 – The Hanged Man. This card is usually representative of a person finding himself / herself (at the moment or in the near future) in a period of distress and personal torment, which might be the result of bad choices from the past. It can be felt that some previous efforts did not end with the desired result, and that the situation can't be controlled any longer. However, this can have a positive role because it leads to a major change in perspective (seeing the world upside-down), and understanding what really matters. If the epiphany is accompanied by positivism and open-mindedness, it will eventually lead to a general sense of peace caused by the success of letting go of the past.

13 – Death. This card marks the transition from a steady, but unfulfilling period to one that might require more effort and responsibilities, but which will be more satisfying in the end. It will seem like death, but one on a spiritual, metaphysical level. A major change is ahead of you, and there is nothing that you should do to stop it. Don't try to avoid the problems that might surround you in this period; these are the ones that will contribute to your change.

14 – Temperance. This card is commonly interpreted as a sign of maturity, perfect balance, and harmony. You must look for these qualities in your life, in order to get to a successful outcome in whatever is disturbing you at the moment. It can also be a sign that you need to make some compromises in a certain area of your life, in order to achieve a universal equilibrium.

15 – The Devil. The main interpretation for this card is that the person might find himself / herself in a position of despair, dissatisfaction, and the feeling of having lost control over a certain aspect in his / her life. Thus, hopelessness and the struggle to get material, palpable achievements can be contradictory in this period. The seeker needs to look beyond all the superficiality in life, and understand that the power to make the needed change is in his / her hands.

16 – The Tower. A highly troubled time is ahead of you. This can be the result of a previous period in which you refused to listen to your inner voice, and ignored your needs and desires. Conflict – even in a violent form – can characterize you at the moment. Thus, a major disruption of your usual habits and routine is expected. However, it's important to accept the changes, and cope with everything new. In the end, when the highest point of the tower is reached, it will be easier to see that all the changes have had a positive outcome, leading you to an enlightened position.

17 – The Star. The star is the sign for inspiration. This means that a period characterized by creativity, positive thinking, faith, and hope will follow. All these will be valid as much for you, as for those around you. At the same time, you might be feeling that you have the power of influence over other people's destinies. Thus, you must be careful to use this power wisely. Be generous and open your heart to the rest of the world.

18 – The Moon. Unlike the star, the moon is a sign for confusion and a general illusionary state. You might not have a very clear understanding of your own emotions and of the entire world surrounding you. The way in which you perceive reality is distorted, and the result of your own fantasies. Although this will be a proper time to use your imagination for creative purposes, be careful not to become the victim of depression, irrational fears, or anxiety.

19 – The Sun. The Sun card is about vitality, good disposition, hope, and achievement of past wishes. This is or will be a productive period in your life (financially, personally and spiritually), so put your trust in your good fate and instincts. This is a good time to again try those things that, in the past, did not have the outcome that you were hoping for.

20 – Judgment. As the name says, an important conclusion, finding, or judgment is ahead of you. However, in this case, the verdict will not come from the outside, but from the inside. You are the one who will finally come to an understanding of a past mistake, which now is the time to be corrected and to start anew. Pay attention to all the signs that you get in this period, and balance them with what you feel on the inside. You need to let go of all regrets and doubts in order to step into the future stage.

21 – The World. Being the last card of the Major Arcana, the World is a sign of completion, a continuous cycle which you might feel in your life. And the series of experiences (in any area of your life) will only end with success, personal accomplishment, and the sense of fulfillment. You might also feel like the period is highly charged with contradictory emotions, but you need to continue in the same way, until everything will become clearer and you will be able to relax.

The Minor Arcana

The Minor Arcana is composed of 56 cards, which can be divided in four large categories: Cups, Wands, Swords, and Pentacles (or Coins). There are 14 cards in each of these categories, and they are similar to those in any normal deck of playing cards: an ace, the middle cards from 1 to 10, and the court cards – the king, queen, knight, and the page. In the following paragraphs, you will learn the most important characteristics of each suit and of the types of cards.

Cups. The cards belonging to this suit are associated with the feminine, the yin from Chinese philosophy, and the corresponding element is that of water. At the same time, these cards are representative of emotions, (usually prevailing over rationality), and they can signify that the person is primarily focused on spirituality and the empirical reality. The needs of the soul – such as always being half in a healthy, steady relationship, for example – are or should be taken into consideration before the most important decisions. As the water constantly flows, reaching parts unknown to the human eye, the person should explore as much in the inside, as in the outside world.

Pentacles. This suit of cards corresponds to the element Earth and the material, worldly reality. The qualities associated with these cards are pragmatism, material gain, personal fulfillment, and satisfaction, but mostly where the needs of the body are concerned. Thus, the physical world is the main source of prosperity and wealth that are so much sought for. At the same time, the cards from this suit correspond to the elements of nature, emphasizing a stronger connection with everything that the natural world offers us for free and in abundance. A strong connection with living nature is also accentuated.

Swords. The Swords are, in a way, at the opposite point from the Cups. Representing the element Air, the Swords are characterized by freedom, open-ness, clarity, and infinite possibilities. The corresponding features are the power of reason and intellect, which predominated over emotion and spirituality. The truth, wisdom, and the actual reality are the most important elements. However, this is not always a positive thing. Anyone who tends to forget about the needs of the soul and heart can suffer certain imbalances. As a consequence, unhappiness, stress, and anxiety can appear over time.

Wands. In Chinese philosophy, the Wands correspond to the masculine, the yang, and represent the element Fire. These elements perfectly describe the constant energy, passion, physical and mental action that are associated with these cards. Creativity, imagination, intuition, the need for adventure, and to know the world through personal experience are the qualities that are the most representative for the Wands. Personal, direct involvement has always been the best option.

Although I presented these cards as being different, and separate from one another, in reality, they all form a single unit – that of the universal world. They can't exist separately and, as you will see in your readings, they must be interpreted together, because the meaning of one card depends on all the other ones from the spread. The first ten cards are easy to interpret, because they are symbols of intensity, and they are in strict connection with the qualities represented by the suits. However, the Court Cards usually need some further clarifications.

The King. This card is representative of all those values that are usually associated with the traditional meaning of masculinity. Always taking the main characteristics of the suit into account, you should interpret this card as a sign of authority, maturity, and decisive choices. Practicality over spirituality and permanent control are also important characteristics that will influence your reading.

The Queen. Contrary to the King's signification, the Queen is the representative for feminine features, and the dominance of the natural world. Just like the traditional interpretation of femininity, the Queen is a sign of emotions, inner feelings, and introspection.

The Knight. The knight is a sign of immaturity, constant energy, playfulness, and sudden changes of perspective. In other words, this card might be a sign of a lost balance, the dominance of one extreme over the other (according to the suit), and the impossibility of differentiating between the good and the evil. Excess, and the denial of supreme authority might bring unhappy outcomes.

The Page. The Page is the least "stable" card. Adventure, spontaneity, and the tendency to abandon everything just from the beginning are the qualities from where you need to start your interpretation of the suit and the final answer of your question.

Chapter 5: All You Need To Know About The Major Arcana

Now that you have an understanding of all the different decks of the tarot, the rest of this book shall draw focus on the most popular deck of all, which is the Rider Waite deck. This deck is divided into two main groups – the Major Arcana and the Minor Arcana.

The Major Arcana cards are also referred to as trump cards, and these are the core cards in the tarot deck. There are a total of 22 cards that make up the Major Arcana. Of these 22 cards, there are twenty one which are numbered, and on which is not. The card that is not numbered is known as the Fool.

When carrying out Tarot Readings, there are those who somethings carry out readings using only the Major Arcana cards. There are a few reasons why this is so. The first reason is based on what these cards actually represent. They can take you through a myriad of stages in your life, such that you are able to gain greater understanding as to what is happening to you. This way, you can learn from your experiences. Second, they seem to tap directly into your human consciousness, and thus, they are able to reveal certain life lessons that you should be going through.

As mentioned in the previous chapters, each of the cards in the tarot tells a story, and to gain a better understanding of each card, it is essential for the card to be studies deeply. With the Major Arcana card, one must look at the total image that they see on each card, and take time to try and understand what the image may actually represent. This requires comprehension of the symbolism that is illustrated on the cards.

Some of the cards in the Major Arcana are direct in the message that they communicate. This is understood once the names of these cards are assessed. Cards with names like Justice and Strength clearly outline their meaning. Once you understand imagery, you will be able to discern which cards are much more personal in what they try to communicate, such as the hermit and the Magician cards. There are also cards that are linked with astronomical heavenly bodies, such as the three cards for the Sun, Moon and Stars. These represent forces that are elusive.

In a typical reading that involves the entire deck, the appearance of a Major Arcana card means that this card is given much more focus, as this highlights that the issues at hand are worthy of significant consideration. The meaning of the cards will change depending on the direction that the card is facing when it is uncovered during a reading. The card could appear to be in the upright position, or it could be upside down which is also known as having a card that is reversed.

The following section will describe the different cards, while also explaining what they mean based on the way that they are uncovered.

The Major Arcana Cards and their Numbers,

0 The Fool

When this card appears in the upright position, it symbolises innocence, as well as spontaneity and beginnings. However, when it is reversed, it reveals recklessness and foolishness, as well as naivety.

Although the number zero should actually mean that there is no value, with the card for the Fool, it is a number that represents infinite potential.

When this card is in reverse, you need to consider any actions you are taking and the subsequent consequences, as it reveals that you have completely disregarded these and are behaving foolishly.

1 The Magician

If this card appears in the upright position in a spread, it represents incredible power, resourcefulness and deep concentration. In the reverse, it reveals a waste of talents, lack of proper planning and manipulation by outer forces.

2 The High Priestess

This is a card that gives off the feeling of serenity at first glance. In the upright position, it represents ones higher power, and the control they hold over the subconscious mind. Then in the reverse, this card is indicative of paying attention, especially to what the inner voice is trying to communicate.

3 The Empress

This card embodies femininity, and is representative of beauty as well as fertility when in the upright position. However, when it is in the revers position, it means that there is something coming in the way of creativity, and that one has lost hold of their independence.

4 The Emperor

Just as you would expect from a real life emperor, this card symbolises authority. The emperor stands out as someone who is firm, solid and dependable. In reverse, it points at a rigid outlook to events, as well as the need to dominate.

5 The Hierophant

This is a card that embodies religion when in the upright position, as well as the need for someone to conform so that they can be identified to a specific group. It also points towards upholding traditions. In reverse, it reveals restriction, or taking the chance to challenge events that are accepted by society.

6 The Lovers

As the name of the card suggests, in the upright position this card is indicative of love and being in alignment. When it appears in reverse, something in one's life lacks harmony and values are being misrepresented.

7 The Chariot

The chariot is used when people go to war, and this card in the upright position points towards a victory and control. When it is in reverse, it points towards the opposite, which is a lack of control as well as the need for aggression.

8 Justice

Being fair and representing truth is what the justice card is all about when it is upright. It looks at being on the right side of the law. Then when it is in reverse, it deals with dishonesty, and also the element of unfairness.

9 The Hermit

When you are going through a soul searching period in your life, where you spend time away from others and have separated yourself, you may uncover the hermit card in the upright position. However, when this card appears in reverse, it indicates that one is isolated, and that they have withdrawn from normal interaction.

10 Wheel of Fortune

This is a card that indicates a period of good luck, when something is about to change in life. The opposite is the case when this card is in reverse, when it then indicates a period of bad luck where everything seems to have slipped through being controllable due to negative forces that are external.

11Strength

Similar to what you would expect from a lion, this card represents courage, and also strength. It reveals that one has compassion for a particular situation when it is in the upright position. In reverse however, it points out weakness, and a period where one doubts something about themselves.

12 The Hanged Man

The hanged man seems to balance on a branch completely upside down, which indicates suspension, as well as someone making a sacrifice. In reverse, it indicates that something has been delayed, or one is taking on the position of a martyr.

13 Death

This card represents certain things coming to an end, or a period of transformation in one's life when it is upright. Should it be in the reverse position, it indicates that a person is not able to move on from a situation, and as such, is resisting any changes that are coming their way.

14 Temperance

When you need to wait for something to occur, this is one card that will help you manage your patience. It reveals that things need to be done with moderation, and indicates that there may a deeper purpose within a situation. When in reverse, it means that one does not have a long term vision and that things in their life are out of balance.

15The Devil

As ominous as this card may sound, it actually deals with matters relating to sexuality as well as focus on material belongings. When this card is in reverse, it is positive as it means that one has broken free from something that previously held them captive and has thus reclaimed their personal power.

16The Tower

This card indicates that something has suddenly changed in life, and may also show an impending disaster. When it appears in reverse, it means that one is afraid of change in their lives, and wants to avoid any disaster that may be coming their way.

17 The Star

The star is a card that points towards hope and renewal, and it also means that one has found the inspiration to face and go through a certain situation when it is upright. If during a reading it appears in reverse, it indicates that one is going through despair, and that they no longer have faith to face a situation.

18 The Moon

The moon shows that one is dealing with their fears and anxieties. When is appears upright in a reading, it connects with the subconscious and also shoes where one may have insecurities. In the reverse position, it indicates a person's unhappiness, as well as situations what may be causing some confusion.

19The Sun

Just as the sun is a celestial body that gives warmth, this card also projects warmth and positivity. It reveals a sense of fun and feelings of vitality when it is presented upright. If it appears in the revers position, it may indicate that a person is going through a short period of depression, or that they do not have success in an area in their lives.

20Judgement

This card reveals actual judgement as well as the possibility of absolution. It may also be the sign of a period of rebirth. However, when it is in the reverse position, it may mean that one has refused to look within themselves to find the answers to a particular situation, or they doubt something about themselves.

21 The World

The final card of the major arcana represents completion and a sense of accomplishment when it appears in an upright position. Then if it is in the reverse position, it means that there is a problem with achieving completion, resulting in a lack of closure for a particular situation.

Chapter 6: Beginning Your First Reading.

The Vocabulary

So, you have your deck but have no idea what to do with them, and don't really remember the cards the conform it. Here's what you should do:

Familiarize yourself with the deck

You need to see the complete deck before you buy it, and then afterwards, when it is officially yours you should go through it once more, twice, and thrice, etc. As much as you can. Take your time, there is no rush here, there is only you and the cards and nothing else.

Observe the imagery, the symbols, and the colors. Analyze if it is a card where an action is being done, or if it is more a sit and wait type of thing. Think about how many people appear on the card and their interactions with each other. Is there any struggle? What is the emotion you see represented in the card? Curiosity? Sadness?

In general, imagine that the card is a picture on an illustrated book and think about what you'd imagine the story to be just from seeing the picture.

Assign or understand the cards' meanings

There are many guidebooks out there that can help with this part of the journey. But, keep in mind, they might be conflicting and have different or opposite meanings for a card. Also, the language might be difficult to understand, hindering your comprehension.

Remember when I mentioned things becoming crutches? Well, books are one of the most common. There are people that constantly go to the guides to see the meaning of a card, or people that think they have this one memorized and want to check.

This is not a subject in school that you need to master and memorize before the final exams come. No one will quiz you or evaluate your knowledge on tarot cards. So, take a deep breath, relax, and start having fun. This is something you're doing for you, not for anyone else, and as such you can take as much time as you need to understand and remember cards' meanings.

If you want a tip: use both books and your intuition for this part. Try to make relations to your everyday life, like the magician reminds you of a particular friend that always leads the group, the emperor reminds you of your father with his sever expression, and the empress of your mom that's always concerned about you and supports you through everything.

One-card Spread

Imagine you're learning a new language, the tarot cards are each word that you're still learning the meaning of. You can't form sentences yet, you're still in the basic word by word level. You're just gaining vocabulary.

To practice your vocabulary, you'll draw a card every day, at the very beginning or at the end, whenever you want, and ask something along the lines of, 'What should I know today?' or 'What message is there for me today?'.

Something that is mostly placed in the present and slightly, just slightly in the future. Then draw a card, and write it down in a notebook, like a sort of diary. Don't panic, no matter what you draw, and don't let it influence the way you live. Just go on with your everyday routine like normal but observe the things you experience and the day's events. This will also help you understand the card's meaning and will deepen your relationship with the deck.

Learning Sentences

Once you've got your vocabulary - your tarot cards, down pat and you have a better comprehension of the card, you'll be ready to start stringing them together into sentences to see how they interact. In other words, slightly more complicated spreads or card formations. Here are two very important ones, that are guaranteed to keep your hands full.

Three-card spread:

Yes, three. Not two, but three. Why three and not two? Because the two-card spread is a **teenie** tiny bit more complicated to understand. So, you lay out three cards, from left to right, one next to the other. Now, the lovely thing about these simple spreads is that the ways to use it are endless. The typical meanings to the card positions are:

Past, present, future.

What helps you, what hinders you, what are your realized and unrealized potentials.

Current situation, challenges, guidance.

What you think, what you feel, what you do.

Strengths, weaknesses, advice.

Mind, body, spirit.

Where you are now, what you really want, how to get there.

Two-card spread:

This spread can also mean anything the person wants it to mean depending on the question asked. You will clear your mind, ask your question or the topic you want to know about, you'll place the first card vertically and then the second one goes horizontally on top of the first. Like a sort of cross. In general, the relationship between the two cards will be of opposition, though the second card can be an aid to the first. The typical meanings are:

Situation and challenge

Aim and blockage

Blockage and solution

Querent and adversary

Ideal and what you're settling for

Situation and extra info.

Please remember that spreads can mean whatever you want them to mean, so the possibilities are endless, limited only by the imagination of the human being. So, the ones mentioned here, are only the tip of the iceberg. There are many more meanings to the card positions and you can find some more in guide books or on the internet.

First few months

Let's combine the things we've covered. In the first month or so (maybe more, maybe less, it's irrelevant and depends on the person; remember there will be no evaluation on this) the newbie, affectionately, should just focus on understanding and developing their relationship with the cards. There is absolutely no need to read guide books before you go through your deck or before you start doing one-card readings.

You might want to consult books once some time has passed, when you've gotten a feel of the cards and what you think they might mean. Not to check you've got it right, there isn't a wrong interpretation, but to gain depth. If you don't agree with whatever meaning the book says a card has then that's alright. No need to force yourself to believe the book. Just keep your meaning and that's it.

The best way to learn is to practice, so do one-card readings even if you don't yet understand the cards completely. As I mentioned before, it will help you gain knowledge. Keeping a journal of the cards you draw, what you think they mean, and the things that happened that day will also increase the depth of your understanding. Then when you feel it is not enough or when you're feeling brave and want to try something new, move on to other simple readings. Again, keeping a journal will help lots, as you can make observations and see things from the outside, so to say. Writing things might help you make connections you hadn't seen.

The other spreads, meaning four, five, or six-card spread, or even the Celtic Cross, a ten-card spread, might look really nice and even seem like a good way to test the things you've learned so far. However, it would be best not to delve into those yet. Don't bite more than you can chew. If you do a more complicated spread, the answers you find might just confuse you and cause harm instead of providing information and advice. Everyone want to grow fast and get to the exciting parts of the matter, but things happen in their own time, and steps shouldn't be skipped.

With that said, feel free to experiment with what you already know. Imagine there is a particular situation or question you want to gain knowledge about, but the spreads and the card position meanings you know don't satisfy you completely or aren't quite what you're looking for. In that case, you can assign new meanings to the card positions. There is nothing wrong with doing that. In fact, most people recommend tarot readers to change things up.

Spreads aren't meant to become crutches either. There is no rule book saying what you can or cannot do. This is not a matter of 'yes or no' or 'wrong or right'. There are no absolute answers when it comes to the tarot. You shouldn't **settle** for anything. Just trust your intuition. If you feel that you need to change the meanings and card positions to gain information or receive advice about your job or family, then do it. Just remember to write down the new card layout and the relationship between cards. That way you won't forget it later on, you might need to use it again.

Chapter 7: Suit Of Swords

The suit of swords usually is associated with conflict, but it can also point toward someone who is forceful or opinionated. The suit is associated with the element of air and sometimes fire, and the zodiac signs associated with it are Libra, Gemini, and Aquarius. They are associated with the mind, thorough processing, and rationality.

Here are the meanings for the suit of swords.

Ace of Swords

Upright, the ace of swords represents someone who will experience a victory, raw power, break-through, and mental clarity. Reversed, it symbolizes someone who will experience a lack of clarity, confusion, and chaos.

Two of Swords

The two of swords upright is a bad omen of someone who will experience indecision, a stalemate, block emotions, and choices. Reversed, the card stands for confusion and information overload. Overall, the two of swords is not a good card to draw at any time.

Three of Swords

The three of swords upright stands for someone who will experience a painful separation, heartbreak, sorry, grief, and rejection. Reversed, the card symbolizes a release from pain and forgiveness.

Four of Swords

The four of swords upright stands for relaxation, contemplation, recuperation, passivity, and rest. Reversed, it stands for a lack of progress and restlessness.

Five of Swords

The five of swords upright stands for tension, conflict, loss, betrayal, and defeat. Reversed, it stands for past resentments and someone who is open to change.

Six of Swords

The six of swords upright represents someone who is regretful and experiencing a rite of passage. Reversed, it signifies someone who is unable to move on and they're carrying a lot of baggage emotionally.

Seven of Swords

The seven of swords upright stands for someone who is deceptive and betrayed. It symbolizes someone who has stealth and wants to get away with something. Reversed, it symbolizes someone who is breaking free of mental challenges.

Eight of Swords

Upright, the eight of swords stands for someone who is self-imposed, isolated, restricted and imprisoned. Reversed, it represents someone who is open to new ideas and perspectives, and experiencing a release.

Nine of Swords

Upright, the nine of swords stands for someone who is having nightmares, is depressed and is feeling anxiety or despair. Reversed, the cards symbolizes someone who is feeling hopeless, depressed and tormented.

Ten of Swords

The ten of swords upright stands for someone who is feeling that they've been stabbed in the back, defeated, betrayed, and thus they feel they've lost and there will be an ending to a relationship. Reversed, the card stands for someone who is recovering, but they still have a fear of ruin and there will be an inevitable end.

Page of Swords

Upright, the page of swords stands for someone who is curious, talkative, energetic, and mentally restless. Reversed, the card stands for someone who is nothing but all talk and no action, and they're very hasty. They also promise things they cannot deliver.

Knight of Swords

The night of swords upright stands for someone who is very hasty, opinionated, communicative, and action-oriented. They don't think before they act. Reversed, the card stands for someone who doesn't care about the rules and will break them if they must. They're very scattered.

Queen of Swords

The queen of swords upright stands for someone who is a quick thinker, organized, perceptive, and independent. Reversed, the card stands for someone who is cold-hearted and over-emotional.

King of Swords

The king of swords is someone who is intellectual, an authority-figure, powerful, and someone who seeks the truth. Reversed, the card symbolizes someone who is abusive, manipulative, and tyrannical.

Chapter 8: Wands

Wands are another name for clubs in the original playing deck and they also stand for the element of Fire and their cards are about creativity and will.

Ace of Wands - Upright: ability, making something, starting something new, idea, great possibilities. Reversed: someone who has no ambition, is always worried about something, and has stopped trying to finish their goals.
Two of Wands - Upright: advancement, eventual preparation, choices and uncovering things. Reversed: scared of unfamiliar, and not knowing what you're doing ahead of time.
Three of Wands - Upright: someone who will experience insight, training, and growth. Reversed: someone who is held back, who will experience things that get in the way of their long and short-term

goals, and has no mental preparedness.
Four of Wands - Upright: parties, home, family, peace and society. Reversed: disruption in communication or unwelcome change.
Five of Wands - Upright: someone who has a rivalry with another or is in an argument, possibly with stress, disagreement, struggle. Reversed: someone who wants to stop fighting by agreeing to disagree. They are distinct.
Six of Wands - Upright: someone who wants to be acknowledged by the public, who wants success and advancement. They are self-assured. Reversed: someone who is pompous and self-absorbed, doesn't believe in themselves, and is dishonored.
Seven of Wands - Upright: someone who has taken on a task or challenge and will show endurance. Reversed: someone who won't go through with it because they feel

overpowered and beaten. They may also be over cautious and possessive in relationships.

Eight of Wands - Upright: movement at a high rate of motion, fast adjustments, air travel, and motion. Reversed: interruption, holding back, and disappointment.

Nine of Wands - Upright: braveness, adjustability, endurance, but a test of your beliefs.

Reversed: overly suspicious, skeptical, and guarding.

Ten of Wands - Upright: anxiety, concern, accountability. Work hard with future success. Reversed: someone trying to avoid duty because they have too much on their plate.

Page of Wands - Upright: excited original nonconformist who is always investigating and uncovering new things. Reversed:

person who expects no outcome and has no guidance will have disappointment to their new beliefs or concepts that they come up with. They will have disappointments to the new things they want to try.

Knight of Wands - Upright: strong emotion, intensity, desire, craving, activity, risky undertaking, and impetuous. Reversed: someone who expects a bad outcome and lacks ambition. Careless, disorganized, discouraged.

Queen of Wands - Upright: caring, energetic, enthusiastic, very persistent. Reversed:
Combative, destructive, insistent, and shy.

King of Wands - Upright: natural born ruler, someone who starts their own business, ambitious, and noble. Reversed: careless, impetuous, heartless, someone who has high predictions for those around them.

Chapter 9: Knowing More About The Minor Arcana Cards

Now that the associations for the major arcana cards were discussed, it's time to delve into the meanings of the minor arcana cards, or the cards that give foresight on the everyday events of a person's life.

What does the Wand signify?

This suit, being associated with the Fire element, is a representation of change. This element is known to give warmth and light; however, if not controlled, it can burn or even destroy. Just like the element, the Wands represents a person's imagination and the desire to create something. This also refers to a person's desire to make their dreams real. When this appears in the client's reading, it may be telling something about their work, career, or ambition.

Just like in the major arcana, each suit in the minor arcana has both positive and negative associations. For Wands, the following can be attributed:

Positive	Negative
Determination, Enthusiasm, Passion	Disappointment, Reckless behavior

Even if the suit has a general meaning, each card that is part of it has their specific meanings, which can be found in this table:

Card	Positive Meaning	Negative Meaning
Ace	Creativity, Fertility, New beginnings,	Greed, Frustration, Overconfidenc

	Originality	e
Two	Partnership, Earned success	Worthless goals, Pride, Futility
Three	Conviction, New ventures, Partnership	Frustration, Lack of nerve, Personality clashes
Four	Completion, New Home, Satisfaction	Decadence, Impatience, Snobbishness
Five	Competitiveness, Conflict, Struggle	Acrimony, being defeated because of devious means, fraud
Six	Fulfillment, Great news, Victory	Anxiety, Delayed news, Suspicion

Seven	Courage, Challenges, Ultimate success	Timidity, Indecisiveness, Lost opportunities
Eight	Action, Activity, Travel	Delays, Impulsive action, Poor judgment
Nine	Self-assurance, Inner strength	Avoidable delays, obstinacy, Suspicion
Ten	Over-commitment, Pressure	Abuse of power, Burden, Deceit
Page	Enthusiastic, Hard-working, Loyal	Impatient, Hyperactive, Spoiled
Knight	Athletic, Unpredictable,	Argumentative, Jealous,

	Vigorous	Violent
Queen	Independent, Practical, Warm	Matriarchal, Overbearing, Vindictive
King	Courageous, Fair, Traditional	Autocratic, Intolerant, Prejudice

What do the Pentacles represent?

The pentacles, being associated with the Earth element, symbolize stability and being grounded. It is also closely related with material wealth, which results in practicality and security. Therefore, it is easy to see that when the Pentacles are present in a reading, it pertains to the individual's financial situation and the accompanying possibilities.

This suit can also have the following associations:

Positive	Negative
Financial prudence, self-worth, stability, success	Financial loss, greed, material obsession

The following refers to the positive and negative keywords associated with each card in this suit:

Card	Positive Meaning	Negative Meaning
Ace	Recognition, Security, Wealth	Greed, Obsession with self, Superficiality
Two	Changing fortunes, Foresight, Journeys	Distractions, Impending trouble, Inconsistency
Three	Prosperity, Recognition,	Bitterness, Criticism,

	Teamwork	Delays
Four	Contentment, Material and emotional security	Material obsession, Indecision, Greed
Five		Financial loss, Hard times, Unemployment
Six	Balance, Charity, Prosperity	Careless money management
Seven	Eventual success, Perseverance, Sustained effort	Failed opportunities, Hopelessness, Money problems brought

		about by the individual
Eight	Change in fortune, Satisfaction	Lack of direction, Wasted opportunities
Nine	Achievement, Material success, Solitude	Financial instability
Ten	Emotional security, Family ties, Inheritance, Wealth	Family restrictions, Financial problems
Page	Careful/conscientious, Loyal, Honorable	Greedy, Impatient, Lazy
Knight	Hardworking, Practical, Truthful	Arrogant, Complacent,

		Lazy
Queen	Compassionate, Down to earth, Responsible with one's finances	Insecure, Materialistic, Suspicious
King	Patient, Practical, Trustworthy	Insensitive, Jealous, Materialistic

What do the Cups signify?

This suit is associated with Water. Just like emotions, Water also has the ability to fill up a container (figuratively, referring to the heart). Emotions are also the "element of life", and can either be poisonous or beneficial to a person. Therefore, it is easy to imply that the Cup closely represents to a person's ability to handle their feelings and emotions.

Some of the positive and negative meanings associated with this suit are the following:

Positive	Negative
Compassion, Contentment, Creativity, Happiness, Love, Understanding	Hate, Jealousy, Lust, Sadness

Just like the other suits, each card in this suit has its own positive and negative association, which can be seen in the table below:

Card	Positive meaning	Negative meaning
Ace	Contentment, Creativity, Faithfulness	Barrenness, Despair, Lost love

Two	Love, Partnership, Understanding	Betrayal, Divorce, Separation
Three	Creativity, Fertility, Happiness	Exploitation, Sex without love
Four	Familiarity, Re-evaluation	Depression, Fatigue, Over-indulgence
Five	Reassessment	Bad luck, Futility, Sense of Loss, Worry
Six	Happy memories, Harmony, The past is shaping the future	Inability to face reality, Nostalgia
Seven	Aspirations, Choice,	Deception in love, Self-

	Imagination	delusion
Eight	Breaking of ties, Change, Development	Dissatisfaction, Restlessness, Unrealistic goals
Nine	Emotional stability, Happiness, Kindliness	Complacency, Finding the fault of others, Vanity
Ten	Commitment, Love, Peace	Anti-social behavior
Page	Caring, Creating, Love	Insecure, Scheming, Selfish
Knight	Artistic or Creative, Enthusiastic, Passionate	Devious, Faithless, Immoral
Queen	Affectionate,	Vain,

	Artistic, Intuitive	Unfaithful, Disloyal
King	Charming, Good Mediator, The Life and Soul of the party	Secretive, Self-centeredness, Disloyalty

What do the Swords mean?

Last on the list of suits of the minor arcane is the Sword. This suit is associated with the element Air and signifies a person's intellect. As such, it is often related with anxiety and stress. This makes this suit quite tricky as the tarot card reader needs to be very good in conveying the meanings of the cards included in this suit.

Generally, this suit can have either of these two meanings:

Positive	Negative

Decisiveness, Ethical principles, Justice, Truth	Animosity, Conflict, Disharmony, Illness, Unhappiness

For the meanings of each card under this suit, refer to the table below:

Card	Positive Meaning	Negative Meaning
Ace	Mental clarity, Necessary change, Victory	Destruction, Injustice, Misuse of power
Two	Equilibrium, Finding friendship despite adversity, Peaceful mind	Deceit, Disharmony, Tension
Three	New	Bitterness, Discord,

	beginnings	Heartache
Four	Tranquility, Withdrawal	Depression, Exile, Isolation
Five	Acceptance	Deceit, Malice, Disloyalty
Six	A breather, Brighter future, A journey	Not being able to face problems, Procrastination
Seven	Diligence	Confusion, Indecision
Eight	Patience	Depression, Getting little rewards from hard work, Restriction
Nine		Misery, Isolation, Disappointment,

		Deception
Ten		Unhappiness, Devastation, Continued Suffering
Page	Truthful, Loyal, Intelligent	Critical, Devious, Sarcastic
Knight	Intelligent, Witty, Courageous	Impulsive, Reckless
Queen	Independent, Intelligent, Perceptive	Insincere
King	Authoritative, Rational, Wise	Bully, Impersonal

How about the court cards?

Each suit in the minor arcana can be divided into the pip (from ace to ten of each suit) and court cards (Page, Knight, Queen, and King). The pip cards are the representation of a person's specific situation or influence, as it can be seen by the theme depicted in each card. However, the court cards do not really "tell a story". So what do they mean?

The court cards specify a person that will exhibit the qualities attributed to them. While the meanings of each court card for every suit are different, the criteria of the person described by the card are the same.

The following will serve as a guide as to who is being referred when any of the court cards are present in a reading:

Page – a male or a female child

Knight – young man aged 35 or less

Queen – woman of any age

King – a man who is more than 35 years of age

How can confusion be prevented in tarot card reading?

One possible problem that beginners experience when providing information is that there are numerous cards as well as meanings for each one. This is obvious, as the tarot deck has 78 cards. Confusion will always be present if there are just too many information that has to be remembered. This confusion becomes more apparent when they start learning the meanings of each card in the minor arcana.

However, this can be prevented by focusing on one suit first before trying to learn of the general and specific meanings of each card in a given suit. Also, before attempting to learn about a new suit, it is recommended that the learned materials are applied in a practice reading along with the major arcana. For example, if the meanings for the Wands are learned first after the major arcana, this suit should be included when doing the next reading. This gradual progression not only enables the tarot card reader to better remember what they've learned, it will also help improve their skills in providing an interpretation using the major and the learned suit in the minor arcana. Eventually, they'll get used to giving an interpretation with all the cards included in their deck.

Chapter 10: How To Read Tarot Spreads

Now, at this point you would like to really know how readings work. Everything from choosing a tarot deck, to spreading the cards and reading the impressions. That's why we are here to provide you a step by step procedure on how to start and become better in tarot readings. Time passes quickly and you won't notice yourself become an expert on this!

Choose Your Deck

As we said earlier, there are thousands of tarot decks being published each year. But as a beginner, you need to own an easy and classic set at first. Advanced decks have a lot of variations from the traditional ones, so steer clear for the moment. We have discussed the top decks in the earlier chapter, we suggest that you choose there for the meantime.

Decide Your Goal

Why do you really want to learn how to read tarot spreads? This needs commitment and it shouldn't be taken so lightly. Real time, effort and money will be poured into learning this art. Once you have decided on what your goal really is, you can become even more dedicated to your goal. Ask yourself how this can help you and how you can help others. Your goals shows your missions, like wanting a deeper perspective and a better grasp on things.

Familiarize Yourself

Once you have your own tarot deck and try shuffling it. When it is shuffled and out of order, try organizing them in place; from Fool up to the kings. When you're done, try shuffling it and arranging it again. What exactly does this do? You get to really know your deck, getting familiar with each character and knowing what their place is. In a short amount of time, your tarot deck will become an extension of who you are.

Understanding Your Tarot Deck

It's not enough that you get a little familiar with the tarot cards, you need to fully memorize and understand them. Your tarot deck normally has 78 cards all in all, 22 of those cards are called major arcana and the rest are called minor arcana. What's the difference?

Major arcana: These tarot cards are cards with images that depict life and all the stages or experiences that people got through. It's like the journey of life put into cards. It all starts with the fool, who is carefree and young until it ends in The

World which represents the end of a person's lifecycle.

Minor Arcana: On the other hand, this set of cards shows the people, feelings, experiences and events that everyone can't help but encounter in their personal Fool's Journey. All the cards here represent, elements which are out of the person's control. The minor arcana kind of represents the common playing cards. It also has suits that have their own elements. Not to mention its very own set of King, Queen, Knight or Jack, there are also Princesses or Pages.

Of course memorizing 78 cards with different depictions and characters will take time. You don't have to rush it, it's not an exam or anything.

A Card a Day

A simple as it sounds, you choose one card a day and pour all your attention to that particular card. Of course you choose another card for the next day. Once you grab that card, write down your impressions on the design, the name or the card itself. You can even conduct a little online search for further information.

Really pay attention to all the major and minor detail that the card has, but never forget to look at the card as a whole. It might seem a little bothersome at first, but once you get the hang of it, it's actually really fun.

Studying the Card Combinations

You must understand that the deck may be made up of 78 individual cards, but they are read as a whole. There are tons of different patterns, systems and combinations to make out. First, you can try picking two cards and comparing them for images, locations and other combinations. Of course you can do it with more cards or even the whole deck of you preferred.

Try Telling a Story

Well, tarot readings are basically telling another person their possible past, present and future. You need to try and highlight all the possible influences in the past and be able to understand the situation in order to predict their future. Though you should always remember that nothing in life is certain and prediction can change 100% of the time.

Start Practicing

You can conduct your trial reading by first shuffling the tarot cards and spreading them. Now, you open each one and write down all the impressions that you have on the cards. Look at the pictures, the individual meanings and their combination as a whole. Ask yourself questions of certain situations in the person's life and possible problems that they might be facing. Write down your best conclusion and also all the other possible ones.

Chapter 11: Common Tarot Reading Mistakes

There are several common mistakes that people make when they are reading tarot cards and I would like to go over them in this chapter. If you have made these mistakes in the past do not worry, it happens to almost everyone when they are first starting out simply take note that way you don't have to worry about making these mistakes again.

Don't read the cards more than one time for the same question. This happens often because you may not be confident in your interpretation or you or the seeker may not really be happy with the outcome. For instance if the outcome was not the answer the seeker was looking for they may want another reading. The truth is that this is only going to confuse the seeker if they get a different answer. Read once and leave it alone.

Using too complex of a spread too early on. In the beginning of this book I gave you several spreads you can use. The Celtic spread is a basic spread and I suggest that you use that one when you are first starting out but you also have to understand that each position can change the meaning of the card just a little bit and each of the cards in each spread change the meaning of the other cards as well If you are struggling with a Celtic spread I suggest you do a simple three card spread when starting out and leave the more complicated spreads for when you have more experience.

Always choosing to read on a positive note is also another mistake that many beginners make. Often we do not want to tell people that they are on the wrong path or their relationship is going to fail or they are going to suffer grief so instead of telling what we see in the cards we try to give it a positive spin. Try reading for someone and recording the session leave the spread laid out until after they leave and go back, really look at the cards and ask yourself if what you told them is what you really see. Listen to the recording and go back through the cards, are you really reading the cards or are you telling them what you think they want to hear?

Allowing the seeker to expect you to read their minds. You need to explain to the seeker that if they want the best information you can give them they are going to have to give you all the information concerning a specific question. For example if they are wanting to know if they should continue on with a relationship they need to be able to tell you why they are considering ending the relationship. This is because if you do not have all of the information you may easily overlook something in the cards. Simply explain to them that you are not a mind reader and you need them to understand that, tell them that you simply read the cards and having all the necessary information will help you do so accurately.

You should not allow seekers to spy on others with the cards. The purpose of the cards is to help them make decisions in their own lives if they are seeking information that affects their life it is fine but do not allow them to ask questions such as: Is my boyfriend at work when he says he is.

Some people you will read for will be hoping to get a specific answer from you and they are unwilling to accept any other answer as the truth. In order to avoid this you need to explain to the seeker that the answers do not come from you but they come from the cards. Neither you nor they have any influence on what the cards are going to say and it is important that they accept the answer they receive. This should be done before every reading.

Another common mistake that readers make is that when they read themselves they do not write their question down. This means that most of the time when they do not get the answer they are looking for they will simply tell themselves that this answer pertains to another part of their life that they were thinking about during the reading. In order to prevent this make sure you not only write your question down but you write down all of your feelings that pertain to the question. Focus on the question as you shuffle and deal. This will eliminate any confusion for a reader reading themselves.

Readers also tend to not follow through when they read for themselves. They may feel that the reading was wrong or that they were not focused on the correct question but for whatever reason they don't follow through. If you read yourself and you learn that you need to change your path than you need to follow the cards and change your path.

Depending too much on your little white book is also a common mistake. What I mean by this is that you depend too much on your pages that are telling you the meaning of the cards or the meaning of the position of the cards. I discussed this a little bit in the previous chapter and do suggest that you follow those tips given to you so that you can learn the meaning of the cards as well as the positions.

Allowing good readings to build up your ego or make you think that you have some sort of mystical powers. Remember this is a learned skill and it is only going to take one bad reading for you to remember that there are no psychic powers involved in reading tarot cards.

Once huge mistake that many beginners make is that they will give the outcome according to the cards but they will not offer a way for the person to change the outcome. This makes people feel as if they are stuck in a situation they will not be able to get out of. As a tarot reader you need to understand that your job is not only to read the cards but you are also a therapist of sorts. It is your job to provide counseling to your seeker to help them change negative outcomes.

Not setting boundaries. This is a mistake that almost everyone makes and I myself made. This is when your friends show up and ask you to read them out of the blue, people come to your door without making an appointment and you get emergency reading phone calls. Yes this happens, a friend's boyfriend is late getting home and you get a phone call begging for an emergency reading in the middle of dinner with your family. You have to explain to everyone friends and family included that you are not going to read them whenever they desire, if they set up an appointment you will gladly read them but invading your life is not acceptable.

You also need to make sure that you are not giving any medical or legal advice. Tarot readers are just that, tarot readers. They are not lawyers, they are not doctors and they are not psychiatrists. If you feel that a seeker needs to get medical or legal help you can feel free to tell them that but in no way should they feel as if they can come to you for medical or legal advice. It is important that you explain this before each session begins.

You should never think that you have it all down. There is always going to be something that you can be learning, you will never be the best tarot reader around although you may be the best reader in your town. If you allow yourself to think you know it all you will find that your readings are wrong and you will quickly begin to understand that you in fact do not know everything there is to know about reading tarot cards.

 Do not allow a seeker to ask you to make a decision for them. You are simply there to read the cards, you may have as much information about the situation as the seeker could or would provide for you but you are not in the situation and it is not your decision to make. Tarot cards are used to give an answer to the person who is to make the decision, the seeker. If a seeker asks you to make a decision for them simply tell them that it is not your decision to make. If they ask you what you would do in their situation simply state that you do not have enough information to give them your opinion and reiterate that it is their decision to make.

Finally you need to make sure that you are pacing yourself. Do not try to learn everything there is to know about tarot cards, spreads or readings all at once. This will only confuse and overwhelm you. Instead take some time each day and focus on one area that you would like to learn about. Also make time each day to learn about the cards, the spreads or the position of the cards in the spreads but don't try to do this all at once.

Chapter 12: 10 Top Decks To Consider When Buying Tarot Cards

There are loads of tarot cards out there. Which deck would it be a good idea for you to purchase?

You need to get familiar with the tarot however you have to recognize what kind of deck is most straightforward to utilize. Buying a tarot deck just because can be energizing and overpowering. There are such a large number of astounding decks to look over all things considered.

There are heaps of tarot cards out there. Which deck would it be a good idea for you to purchase?

You need to become familiar with the tarot however you have to comprehend what kind of deck is most straightforward to utilize. Obtaining a tarot deck just because can be energizing and overpowering. There are such a large number of stunning decks to look over all things considered.

Some prepared tarot card perusers figure you shouldn't buy a deck for yourself, however get it as a blessing. I believe it's superbly alright to buy a tarot deck for yourself, who makes every one of those standards in any case?

On the off chance that you feel associated with having another person buy and additionally pick the deck for you, and that is fine yet in the event that you need to take as much time as necessary and discover the tarot deck that feels directly for you and buy it yourself, at that point here you will locate some great decks and the reasons why they may settle on a decent decision.

have an inclination that picking your own tarot cards and in any event, making the buy yourself is enabling, and why not? Your tarot cards will undoubtedly feel like something you can interface with vivaciously for extraordinary readings.

It's an individual buy in any case. Be that as it may, on the off chance that somebody needs to purchase or buy a tarot deck for you as a blessing, recognizing what you really need can make it fun, as well.

There are such a significant number of tarot cards available going from amateur to propel tarot peruser level. You can feel overpowered with such huge numbers of energizing decisions to look over, some tarot cards even have crystal gazing based subjects for zodiac signs, as well.

Every tarot deck accompanies interesting work of art, imagery, and some incorporate a quality friend How-to peruse this tarot deck book.

The vitality you feel about a specific arrangement of tarot cards and their bundling, are everything to think about when chosen what deck you need to put resources into.

I've ventured to concoct a rundown of the absolute most lovely decks out there. Trust me, it's a pittance however. There are even tarot decks that I have been watching, which are still in different phases of creation.

The following is a rundown on 10 staggering Tarot card decks to think about when making your first buy. Maybe you will locate the ideal tarot deck or possibly a few thoughts for what you might want in a deck (and would not).

1. Rider-Waite Tarot Deck

This deck has 78 cards and was initially distributed in 1909 and is viewed as the best quality level for tarot decks, most decks are displayed from this deck. A Great amateur deck, there is a lot of data about how to utilize this deck accessible.

The deck contains profoundly emblematic work of art yet is really fundamental in masterful structure. Simple use to utilize and sold in numerous areas and stages.

2. New Age Gilded Tarot Deck

The Gilded Tarot deck is a 78 card deck by craftsman Ciro Marchetti. This is a lovely dream deck fusing medieval, and even steampunk structure components.

The craftsman utilized both hand-attracted and advanced plans to make this incredible and wonderfully hued deck. This deck is a lively deck displayed off the customary Rider-Waite imagery and would settle on positively an exquisite decision.

3. Renaissance Tarot Deck

This dazzling deck of 78 cards made by craftsman Brian Williams, utilizes Greek god and goddess type figures just as folklore scenes to depict the imagery of tarot. Each card accepts an open door to address the tales and topics of old folklore.

With brilliant contacts through the deck, its bound to access to utilize. The inconspicuous hues and configuration style suggestive of the chronicled craftsmanship style of the Renaissance timespan. Having this deck could want to claim workmanship you could have found in an exhibition hall of antiquated works.

4. Dreams Of Gaia Tarot Deck

The Dreams of Gaia deck contains 81 cards by craftsman Ravynne Phelan, each card is a creative plan dream, with hues joined in solid and energetic detail. The hues utilized permit the cards each exemplify a striking emblematic explanation.

Each card in this deck is past wonderful and I revere the nature topic all through the deck, I truly feel an association with utilizing Tarot along these lines. In the event that this deck associates with you, I figure you would adore it so much you may not ever need to utilize another.

5. Great Tarot Deck

This is a 78 card deck. The cards in this wonderful deck are ethereal and fragile. A fantasy feel to each card with delicate streaming hues and flawless card structures.

I like the vitality of this deck since it offers a positive vibe to every one of the cards, no negative way to deal with these cards, rather it offers positive criticism even to precarious circumstances.

These cards have marvelous clairvoyant symbolism and images established in old occasions. The cards have a straightforward vibe and offer development focused translations.

6. Precious stone Visions Tarot Deck

Precious stone Visions is a deck by craftsman Jennifer Galasso and has 79 cards. This fantastic deck was named for Stevie Nick's collection "Precious stone Visions". This deck has an obscure "clear" type card to show a mysterious component when drawn.

The Crystal Visions deck is based off the Raider Waite deck, utilizing stunningly lovely card structures to pass on the vitality and images of tarot. The pictures are clear and clean plans.

The figures likely to work out, while delightfully drawn, are strong and as tarot ought to be, emblematically full. For example, the Death card has Rider-Waite images and others, for example, runes and the Egyptian ankh.

7. Enormous Tarot Deck

The Cosmic Tarot is a 78 card deck made by craftsman Norbert Losche. I need to state this is the following deck on my own rundown, I planned to have this set one day soon. I discovered it about a year back on Pinterest and have seen them in a nearby shop all the more as of late.

I was struck by both the pictures and vitality of this enormously delightful deck. To me, it has a workmanship deco subject which I have a weakness for at any rate.

The nobility in these cards is apparent to me. I love the hues utilized, while quieted they are as yet exceptional. Certainly a deck for enveloping by a silk scarf.

8. The other way around Tarot Deck

The Vice Versa Tarot deck by two specialists' Massimiliano Filadoro, and Davide Corsi. This is a deck I intend to have, and it vows to be an energizing occasion once I do. This is a remarkable deck, it is included 78 cards yet every card has a completely planned rear, a reflection picture of the front, for an aggregate of 156 pictures.

Interchange implications are remembered for the manual. I wouldn't call this a tenderfoot deck, yet in the event that you love them, recall you don't must have a standard beginning stage on the off chance that you have the enthusiasm to get them, and to make reference to the work of art will be there to fuel your energy en route.

9. ShadowScapes Tarot Deck

Shadow Scapes Tarot Deck was made by craftsman Stephanie Pui-Mun Law. There are 78 cards in this dazzling deck. I possess this specific deck, a blessing from my mother. This deck is stunning with brilliant watercolor pictures.

This deck likewise centers around positive vitality and the friend book is stacked with 78 vaporous stories to go with each card, a profound exercise lies in every story. I have adored utilizing these cards and my readings have been exceptionally adroit, the point of view I am ready to pick up from them is remarkable for my experience.

10. Wild Unknown Tarot Deck

The Wild Unknown Tarot Deck is a 78 card deck by craftsman Kim Krans. This is a truly cool deck of cards. Themed like the Gaia deck with nature as the conspicuous images, rather than painted or hued pictures these cards are increasingly like hand-attracted draws with energetic flies of shading each offering accentuation to the hued bit.

The Wild Unknown is an extremely prominent deck and the tarot cards are straightforward. The friend book is 207 pages of detail on understanding the creature totem images in each card.

Chapter 13: The Symbolical Tarot

The First Septenary: 1 To 6 Arcana: Theogony

PLAN OF WORK

We will currently apply this general law of imagery to every one of the twenty-two significant arcana. We should here ask for the pursuer's cautious consideration, despite the length of the subject viable. We will bend over backward to be as clear as would be prudent, and in this manner, we will initially clarify the plan which we have embraced in the investigation of every one of the cards of the Tarot. First, we will consistently begin from the hieroglyphic sign which has brought forth the Hebrew letter. Court de Gébelin is the creator whom we will counsel essentially upon this subject.

Second, we will clarify from the hieroglyphic character afflict the thoughts that can be logically found in this manner, and which portray the Hebrew letter considered as a sign. Kircher and Fabre d'Olivet are our experts in this work. Third, when we have once characterized the thoughts connoted by the Hebrew letter, we will scan for the use of these thoughts in the emblematic figure of the Tarot. Eliphas Levi, 1 Christian 2 and Barrois 3 will help us in our request.

Fourth, we will decide the significance which must be credited to each card of the Tarot, as indicated by its numerical and symbolical affinities with different cards, in applying to it the general law of imagery. This part of our work is carefully close to home. Fifth we will end the endless supply of the cards by a table outlining all that we have said.

We should caution the pursuer that the examination of the reiterations just will be of no utilization as a method for seeing any card of the Tarot and that the most ideal way will be to pursue the progressive clarifications of each card, with the Tarot before him. We can't end this opening part without insinuating the premise whereupon we have built up the cosmic relations of each card of the Tarot.

One of the most-old books of the Kabalah which we have, the Sepher Yetzirah, 4 says that the three mother letters of the Hebrew letter set to compare with the three universes, the seven twofold with the seven planets, and the twelve straightforward with the twelve indications of the zodiac.5

1 Ritual de la Haute Maggie.

2 Histoire de la Maggie.

3 Dactylologie ou Langage Primitif.

4 Translatée! Into French by Papus.

5 See Franck, La Kabbale, Paris.

Presently in examining the celestial original copy distributed by Christian, we have found that the numbers credited to the planets by the creator of this work precisely compare with the twofold Hebrew letters, and the numbers ascribed to the twelve indications of the zodiac precisely relate with the basic letters. Taking into account that this total understanding between two records of such extraordinary cause merits our genuine consideration, we have along these lines relegated to each letter its galactic correspondence.

THE FIRST CARD OF THE TAROT

ORIGIN OF THE SIGNIFICATION OF ALL THE OTHERS

So far as our work has continued, it pursues that in the event that we know the accurate importance of the main card of the Tarot we can find in this way the meaning of all the others. We can't move toward this subject decisively. The expectation of finding out truly, indeed, pained by the plausibility of committing an error that may have intense outcomes.

The work which we have just achieved will, notwithstanding, empower us to unravel the importance of the imagery of the principal card of the Tarot numerically, yet the general significance just; while we realize that each card must have not one but rather three implications. We should find three adequately broad standards to be applied to each request for human information; for this ought to be the object of the Tarot.

For this situation, we will not surprisingly, resort to those prominent creators who have treated such inquiries from various perspectives, and the understanding between their lessons will give us new light to enlighten our way.

THE POLE HOENE WRONSKI

1 who passed on of craving in suburbia of Paris, was maybe one of the most dominant brains created by the nineteenth century. He declared that he had found the recipe of the total, and his works are obviously a rundown of one of the most raised unions that we have ever observed. We need not talk about the teachings of Wronski, however, we will

just say a couple of words upon the three crude components which go into his law of creation.

Wronski places at the cause of all creation three components, which he assigns by the names,

Fix Element (N. E.)

The component of being (E. B.)

The component of Wisdom (E. W.)

The Neuter Element speaks to the Absolute, Reality coming about because of the complete balance of the two different components by one another. The Element of Wisdom speaks to the innovative workforce with its uncommon attributes, autogenic and suddenness. The Element of Being speaks to the lasting workforce with its qualities, auto proposition, and idleness.

Standard of the Creation or Element of Wisdom.

Standard of Preservation or Element of Being.

Standard of Neutralization or Neuter Element.

These are the three terms whereupon Wronski sets up the establishments of Reality and, thusly, of the considerable number of Systems of creation. We should recall these ends. Fabre d'Olivet, in his, examines upon the main standards which direct everything,

1 Decides the presence of three components, which he names Providence, Destiny and Human Will. Fortune is the standard of supreme Liberty, of the creation of creatures and of things. 1 See Les Vers Dorés de Pythagore and the Histoire Philosophique du Genre Humain.

Fate is the standard of outright need, of the safeguarding of creatures and of things. Finally, the human Will is a fixed rule halfway between the two: the rule of versatility and change in the entirety of their attacks. Presently it isn't important to be profoundly learned so as to see the total understanding which exists between the two creators; the one, Wronski, arrived at these resolutions by arithmetic, the other, d'Olivet, achieved his own by a significant investigation of olden times and its riddles.

The words utilized may fluctuate, however, the thought is in a general sense the equivalent. Wronski s Element of Wisdom (E. W.), the standard of the creation, is a similar thing as the Providence of d Olivet, who in this manner places it as the guideline of the creation. Wronski's Element of Being (E. B), the standard of the perpetual staff, precisely speaks to what d Olivet calls Destiny, and this he finishes up to be the rule of conservation.

In conclusion, d'Olivet's human Will compares in upset focuses on Wronski's Neuter Element. Here then are two altogether different Systems that lead to a similar meaning. Be that as it may, our decisions don't stop here. In the event that we study these three crude standards all the more mindfully, we will discover in the primary: Providence or the Element of Wisdom spoke to in theory by the word God.

Predetermination or Being gives us its personality with the unchanging laws which oversee the Universe. Finally, it doesn't require a lot of concentrates to demonstrate to us that the human Will reacts to man.

This is the premise of all the recondite way of thinking of the people of yore, and net just Wronski and Fabre d'Olivet concur in their decisions regarding this baffling ternary; mysterious science itself declares as its character with these standards by the Naoixth of all its old style. Hermes Trismegistus, the Holy Kabalah, Neoplatonism, the Alchemists through Pythagoras and all the Greek scholars affirm the division of the Great Ail into three substances or universes.

In less remote ages William Postal* gives the key of the Tarot without clarifying it, and the premise of his key is framed by this strange element. Deus, Homo, Rota Trithemius and his student Cornélius Agrippa 2 additionally give us this productive and grand trinity in distress and analogical figures. The Jesuit Kircher 3 portrays this division into three universes as the premise of the Egyptian riddles.

Finally, L. C. de Saint-Martin has composed a book completely dependent on the keys of the Tarot.

Give us a chance to address India upon the law of the Absolute; she answers Triniurti: Brahma, Siva, Vishnu Let us approach China for the extraordinary mystery of her way of thinking, and she will give us the Tri-grams of Fo-HL

1 Clavis.

2 La Philosoqihie Occult.

3 Oedipus Egyptian? Addis ourselves to one of the antiquated starts.

The Egyptians, he will disclose to us Osiris, Isis, ILorus The wash of Greek Cosmogony, the devotee of the study of Egypt, Hesiod, additionally transmits this law to us, and all detachedly affirming Louis Lucas when he States: 1 "I feel that covered up underneath this otherworldly equation of the personality is one of the most significant logical laws that man has ever found." God, Man and the Universe—these are the broadest rules that we can achieve, and they comprise the three implications of the main card of the Tarot.

It stays for us to learn first, regardless of whether these implications react to the crude hieroglyphics, and afterward to decide how far they stretch out through the entire Tarot.

1ST HEBREW LETTER (ALEPH)

ORIG1N OF THE SYMBOLISM OF THE FIRST CARD OF THE TAROT

The Aleph hieroglyphically communicates Man himself as an aggregate solidarity, the ace guideline, leader of the earth. From this hieroglyphic significance are inferred thoughts of the Unity and of the rule which decides it, thoughts which provide for Aleph its incentive as the indication of Power and Stability. Man, or the Microcosm, the Unity and the Principle in every one of the universes, is the importance of the crude hieroglyphics, which, as we see, precisely renders the general thoughts that we have set up.

Be that as it may, mindful thought of tins first card of the Tarot will illuminate us even more. The imagery of the First Card of the Tarot.

THE JUGGLER

On the off chance that you take the main card of the Tarot and inspect it mindfully, you will see that the type of the Juggler delineated upon it relates in all focuses with that of the letter Aleph. In the event that we presently apply to the investigation of this card the standards of the clarification of imagery, as indicated by the Traité Élémentaire de Science Occult, we on the double discover new clarifications of it.

The highest point of the figure is involved by the divine indication of Universal Life co put upon the leader of the Juggler. The base of the figure speaks to the Earth ornamented with its preparations, the Symbol of Nature. Ultimately, the Center is involved by the Man himself, put behind a table secured with jumpers' articles. The privilege and left of the figure are involved by the hands of the Juggler, one of them bowed towards the Earth, the other raised towards Heaven.

The situation of the hands speaks to the two standards, dynamic and aloof, of the Great Ail, and it compares with the two sections Jakin and Bohras of the sanctuary of Solomon and of Freemasonry. Man with one hand looks for God in paradise, with the other he dives beneath, to call up the evil presence to himself, and in this way joins the divine and the insidious in humankind. Along these lines, the Tarot shows us the job of widespread middle person concurred to Adam-Kadmon. On the off chance that we wish to make an outline of the significance of the image, as far as we have now deciphered it.

However, the imagery of this first card of the Tarot doesn't end here. The Juggler holds the wand of the Mage in the left hand, which he raises, and the four extraordinary images of the Tarot are set before him. The Cap, the Sword, the Wand, Pentacles or Talismans, which, as Ave have just observed, precisely compared with the letters of the Tetragrammaton Scepter or Yod, the image of the dynamic Principle prevalent, and of God.

Cup or He, an image of the latent Principle transcendent, or of the Universe. Sword, Cross or Vau, an image of the Equilibrating Principle pre-prominent, or of Man. Pentacles or second He, the cyclic image of Eternity, which joins the three first Principles in a single Whole. From the human perspective, these images compare with the four extraordinary human classes.

The men of Yod, or the Inventors, the Producers. The Nobility of Intellect. The men of He, or the safes of the extraordinary facts found by the men of Yod; the Savants, the Judges. Proficient respectability. The men of Vau, or the watchmen and safeguards of the previous: the Warriors. The honorability of the sword. The men of the second He, the huge number, from which different classes are consistently enrolled: the People.

The four extraordinary images are put upon the table indiscriminately, and Man rules there and must organize them; in the twenty-first arcana, we will discover these images orchestrated in a cross. We definitely realize that the main card of the Tarot is finished by the twenty-initial (21 + 1 = 22), and we see why, if this first card speaks to the Microcosm, the last would speak to the Macrocosm, and the eleventh card, which fills in as the widespread connect to distress the supplements of the Tarot, connotes the Vital reflex Current, which fills in as a connection between the universes. Be that as it may, we should not envision, so we will come back to our first Arcanum.

This image is the first of the entire Tarot, 1 and it bears Unity as its trademark number. The Unity-standard, the starting point of which is impervious to human originations, is put toward the start of all things. We can't recognize the root of this prime reason, which we are substance to attest as per the total law of analogies so all around communicated by Ellipsis Levi—

It is interesting to see, while looking at the situation of the hands of the personages in the Tarot of Marseilles, how regularly this position speaks to the in order letter to which the figure relates, as indicated by Barrois (arrangement of dactylology or crude language). The arcana 1, 2 and 5 are particularly observable in this regard. On the off chance that we can't pursue this Unknown in its standard, it is at any rate simple for us to tail it in its outcomes, and hence our investigation will be just the improvement of the Unity-rule in creation, as per the Cosmogony of old inception.

God, Man and the Universe are, at that point, the three implications of our first card, and we will presently say a couple of words upon the use of this information to the various cards of the pack.

EXPANSION OF THREE PRINCIPLES THROUGH TAROT

The three implications of the primary card individually speak to.

The Creator or Yod.

The Receiver or He.

The Transformer or Vau.

In conclusion, there is a change to the subsequent He, which isn't getting looked at present. In any case, the principal card of the Tarot, taken all in all, speaks to the Creator or Yod; the subsequent card, taken in general, will, in this manner, speak to the Receiver or He, and the third the Transformer or Vau. Every one of them will likewise show the four parts of Yod-he-vau-he in the thought which it communicates.

However, what is valid for the ternary, is likewise valid for the Septenary, with the goal that the principal Septenary, taken in general, will speak to the Creator; the subsequent septenary will speak to the Receiver, and the third the Transformer. Finally, the ternary of change will speak to the arrival of impacts to causes and of results to the rule. Give us a chance to gather this distress by saying

The first septenary speaks to God.

The second septenary „ Man.

The third septenary „ the universe.

In addition, every one of these components is contained in the two others in trouble purposes of their appearances.

GENERAL RECAPITULATION

We have now to restate every one of the usual meanings of the main card in a general figure. As each card in the Tarot will have a similar summarization, we believe that it might be valuable to clarify the plan followed in this game plan. At the leader of the figure will be discovered the Hebrew number and letter of the card; underneath it, the name normally given to the card in the Tarot.

To one side of the figure are the implications in the Three Worlds: Divine, Human, and Natural. Underneath these three meanings is discovered without a doubt the way into each card, as indicated by the table of the transformations of the word Yod-he-vau-he. The Hebrew letters put upon the upper line of this key show the starting point of the card viable; the Hebrew letters put above it demonstrate the accurate significance of the card.

SECOND HEBREW LETTER (BETH)

ROOT OF THE SYMBOLISM OF THE SECOND CARD OF THE TAROT

The Beth hieroglyphically communicates the mouth of man as the organ of discourse. Discourse is simply the generation of man's internal. In this way, Beth communicates that internal identity, focal as a chilling, to which one can resign unafraid of unsettling influence. From these thoughts emerge from a Sanctuary, an untouched houseman and for God. Yet, Beth likewise communicates each generation that radiates from this puzzling retreat, each inner action, and from it issue thoughts of Instruction, of the higher Knowledge, of Law, of Erudition, of mysterious science or Kabalah.

Beth compares with the number 2, and cosmically with the moon. This number has brought forth distress the 'inactive connotations exuded from the Binary; henceforth the thoughts of reflection, of Woman, applied to the Moon comparative with the Sun and to Woman moderately to Man.

THE SECOND CARD OF THE TAROT

THE HIGH PRIESTESS

As we have seen, man is the divine beneficiary; thusly this second card of the Tarot will express distress the thoughts of the first considered contrarily. The main card speaks to a man standing; this, in actuality, bears the figure of a situated lady.

First thought of lack of involvement by the lady and by her position. The man, supplied with every one of the properties of Power, was set amidst Nature. The lady is enhanced with every one of the traits of Authority and influence, and she is set under the yard of the sanctuary of Isis, between two sections. The possibility of a sacred dwelling, of a divine beneficiary.

The two segments, and the arms of the Juggler, express the Positive and the Negative. The lady is delegated with a tiara, surmounted by the lunar bow; she is wrapped in a straightforward cloak falling over her face. On her bosom she bears the sun-powered cross, and upon her knees lies an open book, which she half covers with her mantle. This is the image of Isis, of Nature, whose shroud must not be raised before the profane.

The book demonstrates that the precepts of Isis are covered up, however, she discloses all to the magi the insider facts of the genuine Kabalah and of mysterious science. Give us a chance to appreciate this significant Symbol. The primary card communicated Osiris in the three universes; this second pass on the meaning of Isis, the friend of Osiris.

THIRD HEBREW LETTER (GIMEL)

ROOT OF THE SYMBOLISAI OF THE THIRD CARD OF THE TAROT

The hieroglyphic significance of the letter Gimel is the throat, the hand of man half-shut in the demonstration of a claim. Henceforth it means afflict that encases, all that is empty, a waterway, a fenced-in area. The throat is where the words considered in the mind are shaped, or I may nearly say encapsulated; consequently, the Gimel is the image of the material envelopment of profound structures, of natural age in the entirety of its stages, of the considerable number of thoughts springing from the bodily organs or their activities. Age is simply the secret by which the soul joins itself to an issue, by which the Divine gets Human.

The meaning of Venus-Urania, to which this card compares, is effectively comprehended by the above clarifications.

THE THIRD CARD OF THE TAROT

THE EMPRESS

This image would, in this way, connote thoughts of age, of exemplification in every one of the universes. A lady has seen full-face the individual becomes corporal in the belly of a lady. This lady is spoken to with wings or in the Center of a transmitting sun. The possibility of the otherworldliness of the vivifying Principle of aflicts creatures. She holds a hawk in her correct hand. The bird is the image of the spirit and of life (Holy Spirit).

In the left hand, she bears a staff shaping the visionary indication of Venus. The staff is held in the left hand to demonstrate the uninvolved impact, which Nature, Venus-

TJrania, or the lady practices in the age of creatures. She wears a crown with twelve stars. The indication of the dispersion of the vivifying Principle through every one of the universes, and of the sun through the Zodiac.

The third card of the Tarot shows the consequence of the complementary activity of the two first terms killing each other in one guideline. It is the Neuter Element of Wronski, the premise of each System of the real world. Unquestionably the innovative power, or Osiris, and indisputably the additive power, or Isis, kill themselves in the equilibrated power, which contains in itself the two particular properties of the two first structures.

The innovative standard and the open guideline, having, by their common activity, brought forth the changing rule, a total element is made. The term which currently pursues will relate with the second he of the Sacred Word, and will thus demonstrate the entry from one arrangement to the next.

FOURTH HEBREW LETTER (DALETH)

ROOT OF THE SYMBOLISM OF THE FOURTH CARD OF THE TAROT

The hieroglyphic significance of Death in the belly. It recommends the possibility of an article giving abundant sustenance, the wellspring of future development. The kid is the living connection, which is its lack of bias reunites the restriction of the genders; the Death, accordingly, signifies plenitude springing from division. Light the 1, it is an indication of dynamic creation; yet this creation is the aftereffect of past activities effectively definite, while the starting point of the Unity is distant to human originations.

The Death communicates a creation made by a being as per divine laws. 1 The Death ought to be the picture of the dynamic vivifying guideline of the Universe, Jupiter, and the reflex of the Primal reason.

THE FOURTH CARD OF THE TAROT

THE EMPEROR

This image should express in the dynamic structure trouble that the previous card communicated in the detached. A man situated in profile. The man demonstrates the dynamic; his position, in any case, shows that this action is caused by a predominant Tenn. The first Arcanum, the Juggler, the dynamic supreme, was spoken to Standing, looking to the front; the fourth Arcanum, dynamic relative, is situated in profile. This man holds in his correct hand the staff, the image of age or of Venus Ç.

The staff is held in the correct hand, to show the dynamic impact, which the vivifying standard activities in nature, by resistance to the developmental guideline (Arc. 3). The man is unshaven and wears a cap with twelve 1 See the subsequent He and the investigation upon the number 4. Focuses (six on each side). He is situated upon a cubic stone, winch bears the figure of a falcon. The protective cap demonstrates the standard of the Divine Will in the Universe and its general activity in the production of Life (falcon).

The situation upon the cubic stone demonstrates acknowledgment and trouble in the universes. First, Realization of the Divine Word by the creation. Second, Realization of the thoughts of the animal shared by the fourfold work of the soul Solution. Third, Realization of the activities brought about by the Will. The man's legs are crossed, his body shapes a triangle – fpS Domination of the Spirit over Matter.

Considered all the more mindfully, the figure imitates the image of Jupiter 2 +, who is spoken to by this Card.* the fourth card of the Tarot compares to the subsequent He and thusly bears two very unmistakable angles. It first communicates a term of change joining the primary arrangement (dynamic and latent powers, the connection between the two powers) to the accompanying arrangement; the section from one world to the next.

In any case, it likewise speaks to this term of progress, itself turning into the primary term in the accompanying arrangement. As the accompanying arrangement, taken all in all, is negative comparative with the principal, the fourth image speaks to the dynamic impact of the primary arrangement 1, 2, 3, in the second arrangement 4, 5, 6.

The 4, accordingly, communicates the impressions of the first card in quite a while subtleties. It acts towards the principal arrangement precisely as the subsequent card acted towards the main card.

5th HEBREW LETTER (HE)

ORIGIN OF THE SYMBOLISM OF THE FIFTH CARD OF THE TAROT

The hieroglyphic importance of He is a goal, breath. It is my goal that life is unremittingly kept up and made. Thus springs the attribution of afflicting that energizes to He. Be that as it may, life practices being, by rendering it not the same as some other; subsequently the attribution of acting naturally to this letter. Be that as it may, the activity of life doesn't stop here.

It is likewise the interceding standard, which connects the material body to the divine soul, similarly, that man joins God and Nature; life is to the man (Dleph) what man is to the universe, pre-famously the intervene rule. Here we discover the starting point of the thoughts of the bond, of the get-together of contradicting standards, of religion, credited to He. This letter is basic; cosmically it compares with the molten indication of the Ram, which it clarifies.

THE FIFTH CARD OF THE TAROT

THE POPE

This image communicates the accompanying thoughts

(First) The possibility of Life, of activity,

(Second) Being,

(Third) The possibility of Reunion.

The Initiate of the riddles of Isis is situated between the two segments of the asylum. He inclines upon a triple cross and makes an indication of Esotericism with his left hand. The triple Cross speaks to the triple Lingam of Indian philosophy; in other words, the infiltration of the Creative power all through the Divine, the Intellectual and the Physical Worlds, which causes afflict the indications of general life to show up (first thought).

The two sections symbolize: on the right, Law; on the left, Liberty to obey and to ignore, the embodiment of Being (second thought). The Initiate wears a tiara. Two delegated men bow at his feet, one dressed in red, and the other in dark. Here we locate the dynamic type of that symbolical which is communicated in latent structure constantly card.

A similar thought of Esotericism, of mystery Instruction, returns; however, the educational cost is currently useful and oral; it never again requires a book (third thought). As we see, this card is the supplement of the second; a similar guideline applies to every one of the cards when the aggregate of their number makes 7.

The Empress is finished by

4+3=7

7 = 28 = 10 = 1

2

The High Priestess is finished by

2 + 5 = 7

1

The Juggler is finished by

1+6 = 7.

4

The Emperor

5

The Pope

6

The Lovers

The fifth card of the Tarot relates to the letter he of the Sacred Word. It is the immediate impression of the fourth Arcanum and the roundabout impression of the second Arcanum. All-inclusive life is the negative side of the vivifying general liquid. Their proportional activity will offer ascent to the all-inclusive fascination or widespread Love spoke to by the sixth Arcanum.

Conclusion

Learning to read Tarot card reading requires both your knowledge and intuition. The insight and guidance you have gained from this book should just be the beginning to learning more about tarot. Your familiarity with The Tarot is the first step in successful Tarot reading. Then, you have to practice it daily in order to master this art of reading the Tarot cards.

Thank you again for downloading this book!

www.ingramcontent.com/pod-product-compliance
Lightning Source LLC
Chambersburg PA
CBHW071433070526
44578CB00001B/92